THE
DANNON
BOOK OF
YOGURT

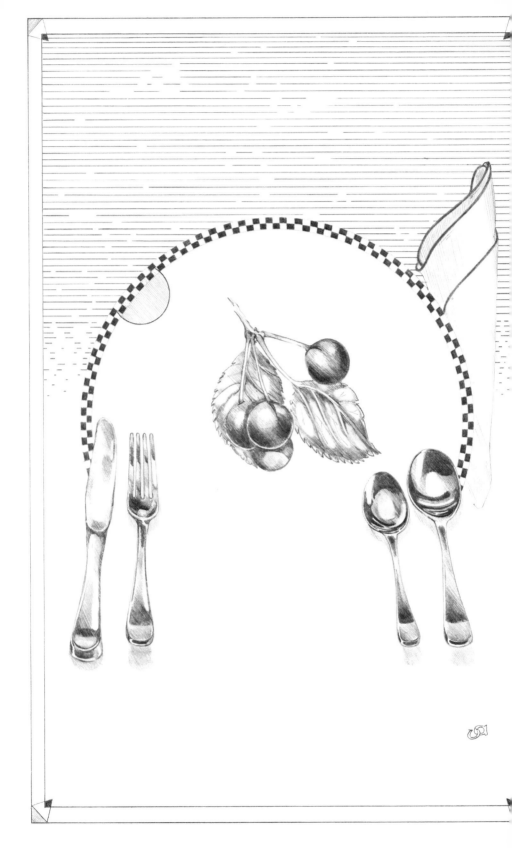

The
DANNON
Book of
YOGURT

by
Sandra Lee Stuart

Illustrations by Vincent Amicosante

CITADEL PRESS · *Secaucus, N.J.*

Acknowledgments   Many, many people contribute to a book like this—suggestion givers, recipe tasters, moral supporters. But I'd like especially to thank the Dannon Company, in general, and Juan and Tim Metzger, in particular, and the wonderfully simpatico Milton Sutton of Marsteller. Thanks, too, to Eileen Gaden Associates for their help and to Paul, who can spot a pun at fifty paces.

SLS

August 1979

Second printing

Copyright © 1979 by Sandra Lee Stuart
All rights reserved
Published by Citadel Press
A division of Lyle Stuart Inc.
120 Enterprise Ave., Secaucus, N.J. 07094
In Canada: George J. McLeod Limited
Don Mills, Ontario

Manufactured in the United States of America

Design by Janet Anderson

Library of Congress Cataloging in Publication Data
Stuart, Sandra Lee.
    The Dannon book of yogurt.

    1.   Yogurt.   2.   Cookery (yogurt)   3.   Low-calorie diet.   I.   Title.
TX380.S78   641.3'7'146   79-19959
ISBN 0-8065-0631-8

CONTENTS

To RJ,
the world's champion yogurt eater,
and to Sarah,
who is no slouch herself

THE
DANNON
BOOK OF
YOGURT

INTRODUCTION

Robert Redford does it. Bob Hope, Willis Reed, Miz Lillian, Princess Grace, Audrey Hepburn, Danny Kaye, Ken Kesey, Maynard Jackson, Sir Laurence Olivier, Burgess Meredith do it.

Ike did it—in the White House.

And so did Nixon.

Baseball's New York Giants did it for the last time in 1954—and 1954 was the last time the Giants won the World Series.

Robert Merrill did it before singing at the Met. Florence Chadwick did it before swimming the English Channel.

And millions and millions of Americans do it.
Do what?
Eat yogurt, naturally.
Yogurt in America is no longer a phenomenon; it's a way of life. Just look at how much is being consumed. In 1969 we ate 143 million pounds of yogurt. In 1977 we gobbled down 612 million!

If you break down who's eating it where, you find that New York and California are doing more than their share of consuming, eating more per capita than any of the other states. Women eat more yogurt than men. People earning more than fifteen thousand dollars a year are twice as likely to indulge than people earning less than five thousand dollars.

But yogurt is being eaten everywhere, in the South, the North, the East, and the West, on transcontinental flights ("Coffee, tea, or yogurt?") and at the U.S. Tennis Association Championships.

It's hardly surprising that yogurt has become such a big favorite. It's healthful, it's reasonable in calories, and it has an outstanding, refreshing taste. The big question is why it took so long to catch on in the United States. A mere thirty years ago yogurt was relegated to health-food stores and ethnic groceries. No more. Today if you can't find yogurt at your grocery store, why even shop there?

This book will answer all your questions such as What is yogurt? Where did it come from? What does it do for you? and What can you do with it? But first, I should own up to something. I have a prejudice about which yogurt I think you should buy.

I think *the* yogurt is Dannon, because of the care taken in its production and delivery. (Dannon yogurt goes from a Dannon plant to the grocery or food outlet in a Dannon truck, ensuring that the delicate containers are handled properly, the Dannon way.) Except for a few places, where I couldn't help it, I've pretty much kept the company name out of it. But you don't have to. Try Dannon—you'll like it.

...AND THEN THERE WAS YOGURT

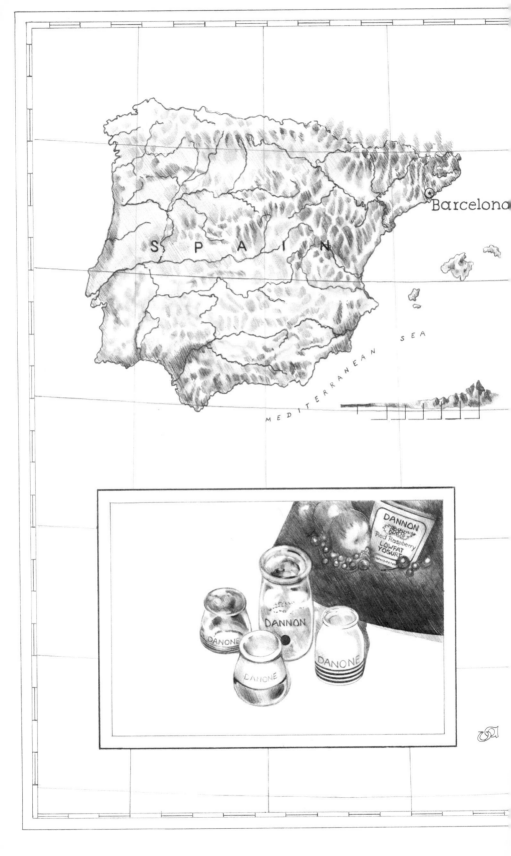

Once upon a time, back when the earth was young and unpolluted, an angel floated—or whatever angels do—around heaven trying to figure out some way to make points with the Boss.

It was not a simple undertaking, considering that the Boss had already taken care of basics—light and darkness, fish and fowl, herbs and spices, man and woman, and the like.

What could one insignificant little angel do to distinguish himself (it might have been a "herself," but who can tell with angels?)? It would have to be something outstanding, something beneficial, something . . . He (or she) had it!

15

The angel would bestow an extraordinarily wonderful gift upon men and women, something to entice them, delight them, and yet do them good, something as close to heavenly perfection as would ever be found on earth.

Into the ear of Abraham, founder of Judaism and all-around good fellow, the angel whispered his gift.

He whispered a recipe, a very special recipe.

He whispered the recipe for yogurt.

Or so the legend goes.

With all due respect for legends, yogurt's appearance on earth in all likelihood predated Abraham. Food historian Reay Tannahill hazards the guess that

> curdled products such as yogurt must have been discovered almost as soon as man learned about milking at the beginning of the neolithic era. A container of milk, left to stand for a few hours, would soon curdle in the climate of the Near East. Depending, among other factors, on temperature and on the type of bacteria floating in the air, the curds might be fine or they might be coarse. The fine variety would develop ultimately into the kind of sharp, refreshing product represented today by yogurt in the Balkans, the taetta of Scandinavia, the dahi of India. Coarse curds, strained off, made the first soft, fresh cheese.

The "discoverer," then, of the tangy-sour milk product yogurt was probably some absentminded Stone Age
person who left a container of yak's milk out overnight,
only to find that a miracle had taken place by morning.

Or the discoverer might have been an equally absentminded nomad who filled his sheep-stomach pouch
with milk and forgot about it. Combine the bacteria
from the sheep pouch, the heat of the hot desert day,
and the chill of the night—and surprise, surprise! The
milk was transformed from its usual liquid state into a
curdy, custardy, sharp and luscious ambrosia that we
call yogurt.

(Actually, it was the Turks who dubbed it yogurt, the
name by which it goes in the United States. However,
the Armenians know it by *madzoon*; the Iranians call it
mast; the Lapps, *pauria*; the Burmese, *tyre*; the Finns,
plimoe; the Chileans, *skuta*; the Sardinians, *gioddu*; and
so on. Call it what you will—yogurt by any name is still
delicious.)

Although the Bible neglects to mention the legend-
ary encounter between Abraham and the angel, it does
make reference now and again to a milk product that
some translators have taken to be yogurt.

What else would Abraham offer the three strangers
when they gave him the great news that little Isaac
would soon be making an appearance? Yogurt, naturally.

And what would Moses partake of on his way to the
Promised Land? You got it—yogurt. (In a more recent
parallel, Diana Nyad trained on yogurt before attempt-

ing to "part the waters" between Cuba and Florida.)
Some years later, Homer wrote about yogurt repasts
in the *Iliad.* Herodotus, the so-called father of history,
mentioned yogurt in his chronicles of the Persian Wars.

Genghis Khan fed yak-milk yogurt to his army,
which may have accounted for their great power and
success at conquering and pillaging.

Marco Polo had the good fortune to be served yogurt
on his China trip. Except for some eastern parts of
Europe, yogurt was not eaten in the West—not, that is,
until a dissolute and rather unscrupulous king of France
introduced it in the sixteenth century.

The king was Francis I, who, when he wasn't getting
into rows and wars with his chief rival, Charles V, was
living the good life of a Renaissance monarch. This
good life certainly contributed to Francis' bad health.

What was a sickly French king to do in the 1500s?
There was no Mayo Clinic or Massachusetts General,
not even a reliable neighborhood druggist. On the con-
trary, the doctors of the day, with their standard advice
of "Let two pints of blood and call me in the morning,"
were best avoided.

What Francis did do was send for a wizened old
sorcerer–medicine man who had built a reputation for
himself in Constantinople. The man was supposed to
have some cure-all tonic that was guaranteed or your
money back.

Francis schlepped the "doctor" up from Turkey, paid
him a kingly sum, and took the tonic—then took some
more because it tasted so great. Within days Francis had

risen from what he had thought would be his deathbed.

To show his heartfelt appreciation, the king dubbed the miraculous tonic *le lait de vie eternelle*, "the milk of eternal life." It was, however, just good, delicious yogurt.

In all likelihood, just about any change in his deca-dently rich, poorly balanced diet would have got Fran-cis out of his "deathbed." Whether yogurt can take full credit is questionable. But it sure beats a sugar pill.

Despite King Francis' endorsement, yogurt con-tinued to have only limited appeal in Europe. Pockets of people here and groups of people there were lucky enough to have it as part of their diet, but most of western Europe didn't know what it was missing.

Skip forward a few centuries. It's 1845 in the Ukrai-nian city of Kharkov. It's here that Elie Metchnikoff was born.

Metchnikoff earned his place in history books through his work in medicine and physiology, for which he won a Nobel Prize in 1908. He carved another niche for himself by drawing attention to yogurt through his work and research on longevity.

What first got Metchnikoff thinking of yogurt and longevity together was a trip he took to Bulgaria at the turn of the century. There he was sitting in a country field, watching some very old women working hard and briskly nearby. What caused these women to live so long and in such good health? he wondered. Could it have something to do with that unfamiliar food they ate in such great quantities? Could yogurt be a factor—

maybe even *the* factor—that contributed to their active lives?

Later when he took up the research in earnest, the scientist postulated that yogurt was instrumental in keeping harmful bacilli out of the large intestines. He believed these bacilli caused hardening of the arteries. In his book *The Prolongation of Life* he maintained, "A man is as old as his arteries." However, Metchnikoff never proved his theories to the satisfaction of the rest of the scientific world.

Whether Metchnikoff's theories were right or wrong, they did make people eager to try the alleged elixir. But more on those theories later.

Another yogurt devotee was a Spaniard named Isaac Carasso. In 1919, Carasso established the first commercial yogurt company. He opened his plant outside Barcelona, importing yogurt cultures from Bulgaria and from the Pasteur Institute in Paris, where Metchnikoff had done his experimenting.

Carasso called his tasty product the Dessert of Happy Digestion and sold it primarily through pharmacies.

He did so well with his company that in 1926 he opened a French branch, putting his son Daniel in charge. As long as his son was in charge, it seemed fitting that the product be named after him. Hence, Danone was born.

The French branch did its own share of prospering, but as the ominous whispers of war crescendoed to shouts, France became less and less a safe place to conduct business. With his father's death, Daniel chose to leave Europe for the United States.

After preparations for the trip were made, Daniel Carasso went to say good-bye to some good friends, a Swiss family living in Spain. They were the Metzgers—Joe, Cary, their son, Juan, and their daughter, Miriam.

At the end of the stay, Juan escorted the Carasso family to the train station. What followed was like a Hollywood script.

Leave-taking. Conductor shouts, "All aboard!" Steam billows up from the tracks.

Carasso leans out of the window. "Juan!" he calls. "Juan, if you ever get to the United States, come see me and we'll make yogurt together."

Train pulls out of the station. Fade-out. Cut and print.

A year later, in 1942, Joe and Juan Metzger did follow Carasso to New York, and they did begin to make yogurt together.

When yogurt and the Metzgers got together, it was lucky happenstance for both. In Europe, Joe Metzger had been a business executive and had little connection with the product he would become "king" of. However, what Joe Metzger didn't know, Daniel Carasso did.

Danone, anglicized to Dannon, set up its first headquarters in a tiny plant in the Bronx and set about to make yogurt an American favorite.

Dannon in no way brought yogurt to the New World.

21

That honor goes to a couple of mysterious Turks who crossed the Atlantic in 1784. Nor was Dannon the first American yogurt manufacturer. A Greek family in the Bronx made and sold yogurt during the 1930s. An Armenian family in Andover, Massachusetts, distributed their yogurt as far south as Mulberry Street in New York City, where there was an Armenian population. A group of Trappist monks helped found the Rosell Bacteriological Institute in Canada, which began supplying yogurt cultures to various small American companies scattered across the country.

Dannon, however, was the breakthrough company, the company that brought yogurt from being exclusively an ethnic delight and food faddists' fare to college cafeterias, board rooms, and the dinner trays of many international airlines.

In those first Bronx days, Dannon produced a mere two hundred jars a day. (They were sold for nine cents, plus a three-cent deposit for the glass jar.) The company's primary customers were Turks, Greeks, and others of eastern-European background, all of whom use yogurt in their cooking.

But with the end of World War II, big changes were in the offing. For one thing, Daniel Carasso began expending his energy reorganizing Danone in France. Finally in 1951, he officially returned to Europe.

But the biggest change came in the yogurt itself. Juan had been charged with creating an American market for Dannon. But yogurt was too alien, too offbeat for the American tastebuds. Something had to be done to make it more acceptable to the American sweet-freak palate. Europeans would cut the tartness by sprinkling a bit of sugar on each spoonful of plain yogurt. But to get Americans to do that would take explanation and education.

In 1947 Dannon found an answer, introducing strawberry preserves to yogurt. (Strawberry was chosen because that was the favorite fruit flavor in ice cream.) To this day strawberry is the company's biggest seller. In 1952 Dannon started selling orange-flavored yogurt, followed by vanilla in 1953. Today Dannon sells fourteen flavors besides plain.

It now seemed that Dannon had what the public wanted. The next problem was letting the public know that yogurt was what it wanted. It wasn't especially easy.

Be it ever so good, yogurt was an entirely new product for most Americans. When Clarence Birdseye, or whoever it was, froze the first baby pea and then tried to sell it, the public at least knew what a pea was, even though it was being hawked in a new package. Yogurt, on the other hand, was foreign, exotic. Would it ever "play in Peoria"?

Yogurt was so little known, in fact, that the following incident, which seems incredible today, actually happened.

In the 1930s, a young man called on a young woman for their first date. When he picked her up, he asked her whether she liked yogurt.

"Yogurt?" she squealed, not having the slightest idea

what it was. "Yogurt? How dare you!" And she slugged the young man for the suspected affront.

("It took three years, fifteen days, and ten hours before I got him to marry me," the sweet young woman was to remember.)

People simply didn't know what yogurt was, or if they did, they thought it was some kind of weirdo food. Juan Metzger turned to an ad agency for help.

As he was to explain,

> *Yogurt is a new food. The yogurt business is a tough one. People live very happily without it. The taste and the name are screwy. In our minds we have preempted what we eat at different hours of the day.*
>
> *At breakfast you don't eat ice cream and apple pie. You don't have soup or Chinese food. In your mind you have eliminated what you are not going to eat. So it was difficult to get people to fit yogurt into their eating pattern. I had to say, "Here is yogurt. Eat it." And the person would say, "Why should I? When?"*

The Zlowe Company, an ad agency, now merged into Marsteller, Inc., did some market research and found that basically three groups of people were eating yogurt: (1) health-conscious Americans who were very choosy about what they ate (food faddists fell into this category); (2) Americans who had tried yogurt while visiting Europe; (3) European-born Americans.

Obviously, Dannon wanted to expand that market. Get people to taste yogurt and there was a chance, they felt. Most of the early advertising budgets (the first in 1942 was for only ten thousand dollars) went for demonstrations at food stores and markets. Free tastes for the uninitiated.

It was found that for every ten people who tasted the plain, there'd be one convert. For every ten tasting the strawberry, there were three and a half.

Then Dannon started advertising. Most of the early ads were health-oriented, despite some food purists who sniffed at the idea of mixing fruit preserves with yogurt.

"Dannon the real yogurt . . . it's healthful . . . it's deliciously different," read one ad.

Next came radio advertisements, first on "The Alfred McCann Show" to reach the food-conscious people and then on "The Mary Margaret McBride Show" for the average housewife.

Then the campaign got two tremendous boosts. One was from Gaylord Hauser, who extolled yogurt's virtues in his book *Look Younger, Live Longer*. The other was a laudatory article in *Reader's Digest* in 1951.

After almost ten years of financial statements that reflected little success, Dannon was doing well— except for one annoying thing. Maybe it was the "screwy" name or maybe it was just because people make fun of things they are not familiar with. In any case, yogurt had become a sure-fire rib-tickling, laugh-provoking catchword for jokes.

"I flew over Greenland," Bob Hope quipped, "and it looked like one big yogurt."

"Did you hear about the ninety-seven-year-old

25

it's Healthful . . .
it's Deliciously *Different*

Eat **DANNON** *real yogurt* every day

woman who ate yogurt every day? She died, but the baby lived."

In one week the Metzgers counted twenty-four yogurt jokes on radio and television. It got so that one health-food-shop owner lamented, "Everybody talks about yogurt, but who buys it, who eats it?"

In the 1950s, Dannon chose to fight laughter with laughter. Its advertisements took the playful approach, as Milton Sutton, of the Marsteller agency, explained, "to make it more consistent with American attitudes. We wanted to avoid extravagant health claims. We didn't want it to be a fringe food."

To which Juan Metzger would add, "People attribute properties to [yogurt]. The greatest part of our effort is devoted to telling them simply that it is a wholesome food that tastes good and urging them to try it."

What Americans began to hear were:

WOMAN: Jim and I have always enjoyed eating Dannon yogurt. Today we still look and feel like newlyweds.

ANNOUNCER: That's wonderful. Still acting like newlyweds because of Dannon Yogurt! And how long have you been married?

WOMAN: About a week.

ANNOUNCER: If you want to look like a bride forever . . . it's all right with us. But the real reason most people eat Dannon Yogurt is—they like it!

and

MAN: I'm a long-distance runner. I used to come in last

all the time. Then the coach made me eat Dannon
Yogurt regularly. Now I always breeze in first. . . .
ANNOUNCER: Dannon Yogurt got you in top condi-
tion?
MAN: No. I take short cuts.
and
YOUNG WOMAN *(after explaining she never looked good
in a bathing suit)*: Then Dannon Yogurt came into my
life. Now every time I go into the water I am sur-
rounded by handsome lifeguards.
ANNOUNCER: Is that because Dannon Yogurt gave you
a sensational figure?
YOUNG WOMAN: No. It's because I can't swim.

The ads made people smile, made them laugh, made
them go out and buy yogurt, and in one case, made
them write letters. One ad, an attempt to counter a
competitor's price cutting, read, "There are 3 reasons
why Dannon is America's best-selling yogurt. The 1st
reason is quality. . . ." The ad sent a lot of people to
the post office. They wanted to know the other two
reasons!

The most famous Dannon ad is probably the recent
Soviet Georgian one.

It was the brainchild of Peter Lubalin, creative direc-
tor of Marsteller, who came up with the approach after
reading a 1973 *National Geographic* article. It was an
article on certain long-lived Bulgarians and Soviet
Georgians, their lifestyles, their work habits. Casually

mentioned, in among a lot of other things, was the fact that these people happened to eat yogurt.

It seemed a natural for an ad campaign. So producer Arlene Hoffman was dispatched to the Soviet Union to find a 90-year-old with a living parent. She compromised with Bagrat Topagua, an 89-year-old with a 114-year-old mother.

The ad agency had surprisingly little trouble getting its very capitalistic undertaking okayed by the Soviet government. The real problem came at shooting time.

As Lubalin explained, "After a shot the whole collective farm would come and sit down and we'd have a feast. The head of the farm would line up six or eight glasses of Stolichnaya and start toasting." They'd toast anything and everything—friendship forever, Mother Russia, the stars and stripes, presidents, chairmen, and the Politburo. As one toast was downed, the Vodka Patrol, women carrying vodka bottles, would refill the glasses.

"I don't exaggerate," Lubalin said, "when I tell you we each drank a good part of a bottle of vodka with the morning banquet and the rest of the bottle with the evening banquet. We did the morning shots sober; the afternoon sessions, forget it."

But somehow the commercials were finished and Bagrat Topagua went on to American media fame. He even has his own fan clubs now.

To say that marketing yogurt in the United States has been a success is a gross understatement. True, yogurt is

29

not in every refrigerator; still, the number of people eating it today, as compared with thirty years ago, compose a marketing miracle.

In 1942 Dannon produced two hundred thousand containers.

In 1967, Americans ate one hundred million containers. By 1972 that had jumped to five hundred million.

From that first Bronx plant with its six employees, Dannon has expanded to six plants—one each in Long Island City, Ridgefield, New Jersey, Miami, Florida, and Fort Worth, Texas, and two plants in Minster, Ohio, a tiny town fifty miles north of Dayton. (Minster could correctly be called the Yogurt Capital of the World, since more yogurt is produced there than anywhere else in the western hemisphere.)

Yogurt, certainly a food of all ages, is coming into its own in the United States—and about time.

Yogurt is so delightful, so good, that it would be easy to believe that an angel really did whisper into Abraham's ear.

THE WHAT
AND HOW OF
YOGURT

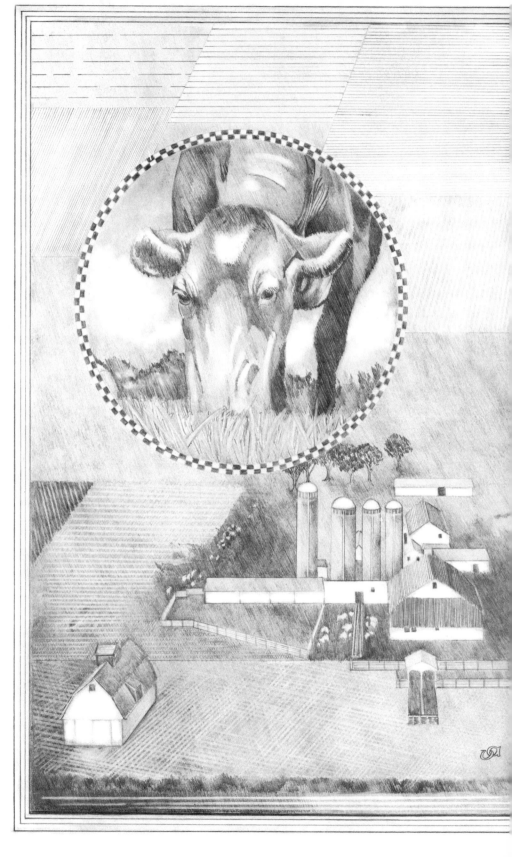

If you're about to introduce an uninitiated and be-nighted friend to the delight of yogurt, it might be best not to detail precisely what yogurt is.

Let the until-now-deprived friend taste its cool tangi-ness. Let him or her savor the lusciousness, become totally addicted.

Once you've made a grateful convert—and if your chum insists—then you can explain exactly how milk becomes yogurt.

Granted the end result is great. But in small print, it might not read too well.

Yogurt, if you're going to get technical, is milk that has been soured by a couple of microorganisms.

Before you panic and reach for a stomach pump,

think back to Biology 101. There are "good" bacteria and there are "bad." Yogurt bacteria—*Lactobacillus bulgaricus* and *Streptococcus thermophilus,* or *Lacto b.* and *Strepto t.* for short—are quite definitely in the first category.

The rod-shaped *Lacto. b.* and the spherelike *Strepto t.* are found naturally in raw milk. Although milk is one of Nature's better foods, it takes humankind to "improve" it and make yogurt.

The alchemy that turns milk into Dannon yogurt takes place in steel-shiny, dial-covered, pipe-filled, super-modern plants, not unlike NASA Mission Control.

Changing lactose—that's milk sugar—into lactic acid and then having enzymes work to coagulate milk protein (what yogurt-making is all about) is a multistep procedure that must be conducted with the efficiency and precision of a moon shot.

It begins where else but in the dairy. Fresh, fresh milk gets trucked from there to yogurt plants before the morning paper is off the press.

The milk is stored in gargantuan outside tanks, which hold up to sixty thousand pounds, until it is time for it to flow into the plant.

In step one, the milk is warmed to 140 degrees Fahrenheit in large stainless-steel vats, where nonfat-dry-milk solids are added for consistency, stability, and extra protein.

In step two, the milk is homogenized—that is, the fat

particles are finely divided so the cream won't separate from the rest of the milk.

In step three, the milk is pasteurized—heated to between 142 and 145 degrees to kill unfriendly germs.

In step four, the milk is cooled to 110 degrees so that in step five the "good" bacteria may be introduced—inoculated—into the milk.

After some shaking to distribute the cultures evenly, the inoculated liquid is piped into a filling machine, which dispenses it into the familiar eight-ounce containers. If the milk is destined to be a fruit yogurt, preserves are put in the containers first. Capped and stamped with a twenty-one-day expiration date, the containers are wheeleed into a 110-degree-Fahrenheit incubation room for about three hours. There, *Lacto b.* and *Strepto t.* get down to business.

When, presto-chango, bossy's liquid is custardy and delicious—as someone once put it, "sour milk with a college education"—the containers are refrigerated to stop further fermentation. Refrigerated trucks then carry them to grocery stores, restaurants, and other food outlets.

The whole process is carefully monitored by specialists. It now takes one minute for the same amount of yogurt to "come down the line" as was produced in one week at the old Long Island City plant.

But despite all the new technological skills and devices, yogurt making, at least at Dannon, is still done with the old-time methods—homogenization and pasteurization first, inoculation second, and incubation in individual containers.

There is controversy now over changes some companies have introduced in yogurt making. Some people doubt that the end product of certain brands should even be called yogurt.

Manfred Kroger, professor of food sciences at Pennsylvania State University, decries the new technique of a second pasteurization after inoculation. He calls it a corruption of the product.

"This means," he has written, "that after the time-consuming culturing or fermentation step that makes yogurt what it is, the product would be heat-sterilized or pasteurized. Such heating would destroy the yogurt bacteria . . . [while increasing] the length of time yogurt can be stored."

This new technique, then, is used to give the product a longer shelf life while enabling it to keep the "natural" label. (Swiss-style, or premixed, yogurt is often pasteurized a second time or preservatives are added to prolong shelf life.)

The federal Food and Drug Administration has been contemplating a regulation that would allow these "yogurts"—some people argue that they are only pseudo-yogurts—to continue to carry the centuries-honored name but with a notice on the label reading, "Heat-treated after culturing."

In the words of the FDA, "The Commissioner believes that it is in the best interests of the consumer to preserve the food in its traditional form, i.e., containing live microorganisms."

Pending action on this regulation, there is a home test you might try if you're curious about whether a certain brand of yogurt contains active cultures. (Dannon does, and says so right on its label.)

Combine two tablespoons of plain yogurt with a cup of warmed milk. Leave the mixture overnight in a warm spot, such as over your pilot light if you have a gas stove. By morning the milk should have begun to thicken if the yogurt contained live cultures.

A second matter of contention among yogurt makers is where incubation should take place—in individual containers or in a large vat. The drawback of the large-vat method is that although it is cheaper, yogurt doesn't transfer well to smaller containers once it is custardy. It loses consistency. To compensate, the large-vat manufacturers add something to tighten the yogurt. All fine and good, but why add anything if it's not necessary? Why not keep the yogurt in its purest form?

Which brings us to the touchy and complicated question of "natural" and "all natural" and in some cases, "almost natural." "All natural" merely means that nothing *artificial* has been added. It doesn't mean that nothing at all has been added. Such items as starch and coloring might have been stuck into the yogurt. Check your label.

Even a label won't help you, however, when a company doesn't put preservatives into the yogurt but does put them into the preserves. Legally it doesn't have to mention that on the yogurt container.

And watch out for those Swiss (premixed) styles that have additives to keep fruit in suspension. Fruit, being heavier than yogurt, would tend to fall to the bottom. If you think that the color of some of those Swiss styles is too vivid to be real, you're probably right. Coloring is used. Yogurts that are "rippled" with fruit generally use potassium sorbate as a preservative.

If you are of the mind, as one frozen yogurteer is, that "God made chemicals, so why not use them?" none of this makes a dash of difference. On the other hand, should you be one to shudder at the glop that goes into so many food products, and should you be afraid of this assault on your body—let the eater beware. Read the label and buy products you can trust.

Yogurt is just too good to tamper with. Know what you're buying. Know what you're eating.

GOOD
HEALTH
AND GOOD
YOGURT

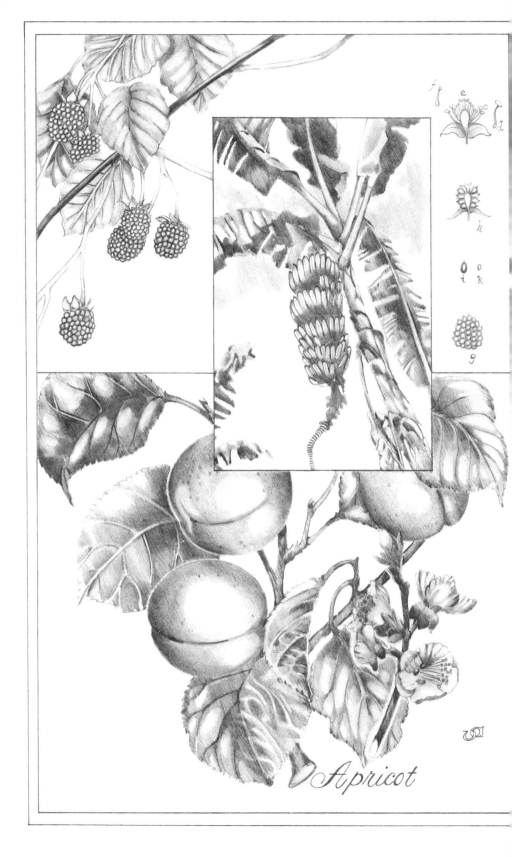

f g e c
d

h

i o
k

g

Apricot

Somewhere, at some time, someone has believed that eating yogurt would cure:

insomnia, impotence, halitosis, hepatitis, dandruff, Montezuma's revenge, constipation, kidney stones, gallstones, arthritis, migraines, wrinkles, thinning hair, food poisoning, ulcers, sunburn.

Yogurt has been thought of for centuries as a wonder food. Pliny the Elder, the prolific Roman naturalist with a penchant for collecting secondhand information, wrote that the ancient Assyrians preached that *lebany*—their name for yogurt—was divine and could cure almost anything from bee bites to bursitis.

Arabic, Persian, Greek, and Hindu physicians held to the conviction that large doses of yogurt prevented epidemics. Persian women slopped it on their faces to smooth out wrinkles. Turks mix in flowerbuds before putting it on their foreheads as a cure for insomnia.

Indians think that yogurt for breakfast restores balance to the brain. And syndicated columnist Bert Bacharach (father of composer Burt Bacharach) passed along the theory that yogurt at night prevents a hangover in the morning.

Yogurt is such a good and wholesome food that it's little wonder that such an impressive collection of folklore and beliefs arose around it. It's pure and it's simple, and it's good for you, and at long last modern science is beginning to study it seriously.

After centuries of being considered miraculous, a cure-all, beneficial to your health, yogurt in recent years has been burdened with anti-myth myths. Some extremists debunk the yogurt legends to such an extent that they claim that eating yogurt is not beneficial to your health at all. Not so. Yogurt research is still in progress, but some things are known.

Before anything else, it can be said unequivocally that yogurt is a highly nutritious food and a fine source of vitamins and minerals.

Both milk and yogurt are sources of valuable nutrients. Comparing the two, fortified milk is a slightly better source of magnesium, folic acid, and vitamins A and C. But yogurt wins in the categories of protein, calcium, phosphorus, zinc, thiamin, niacin, and ribo-flavin.

Check out your plain-yogurt container. There on its side is the story.

Here's how plain Dannon yogurt stacks up against flavored and fruit:

Serving size: one 8-oz. cup (227 grams).

	Plain Yogurt	Flavored Yogurt (coffee, lemon, vanilla)	Fruit Yogurt (strawberry, cherry, honey, etc.)
Calories	150	200	260
Protein	12 grams	11 grams	10 grams
Carbohydrate	17 grams	32 grams	49 grams
Fat	4 grams	4 grams	3 grams
Cholesterol†			
mg. per serving	15 milligrams	10–15 milligrams	15–20 milligrams
mg. per 100 gm.	5 milligrams	5 milligrams	5–10 milligrams
Sodium			
mg. per serving	235 milligrams	215–255 milligrams	200–250 milligrams
mg. per 100 gm.	105 milligrams	95–110 milligrams	90–110 milligrams

Percentage of U.S. Recommended
Daily Allowances (U.S. RDA)

Protein	30	25	20
Vitamin A	2	2	*
Vitamin C	*	*	*
Thiamine	4	4	2
Riboflavin (B$_2$)	30	20	20
Niacin	*	*	*
Calcium	40	35	35
Iron	*	*	*
Vitamin B$_6$	4	4	2
Vitamin B$_{12}$	20	20	15
Phosphorus	35	30	25
Magnesium	10	10	10
Zinc	8	8	6
Pantothenic Acid	10	8	6

*Contains less than 2% of the U.S. RDA of these nutrients.
†This information on cholesterol content is provided for individuals who, on the advice of a physician, are modifying their dietary intake of cholesterol.

44

Not long ago, most Americans would have yawned at this information, feeling that it was of interest only to Olympic athletes and little gray-haired ladies teaching home economics.

A mere twenty years ago, a European nutrition expert dismissed our nation's eating habits with, "No Americans, except for a few dedicated faddists, will eat for the simple reason that it is good for them. You have to convince them it is primarily sociable and fashionable, and only incidentally will help them feel better and live longer."

Times and eating habits are achanging in our great land of junk food and empty calories. The old saw "You are what you eat" is beginning to make more and more sense to more and more people.

Those recommended daily allowances (RDAs) are getting deserved attention now. As they should. And vitamins play an important role in how you feel and how you function.

Start with protein.

Besides being essential for the growth, maintenance, and repair of the body's cells, it is used by enzymes and hormones to regulate the body's processes, by antibodies in fighting off infection and disease, and in the structure of hemoglobin.

The body can't manufacture protein as it can some substances. Protein must be supplied. As you can see by the yogurt label, an eight-ounce cup of plain yogurt supplies 30 percent of your recommended daily allowance.

The body uses riboflavin, or vitamin B_2, to help convert not only carbohydrates, but also protein and fats, to energy. Riboflavin is needed in the production of new tissues and keeps your skin healthy—especially the skin around the mouth, nose, and eyes.

Calcium is essential for healthy teeth and bones, not to mention healthy nerves and muscles, and in blood clotting and the healing of wounds and broken bones.

Vitamin B_{12} functions in the production of red blood cells in the bone marrow, in building new protein, and in the normal functioning of nerve tissue.

The body uses phosphorus with calcium for healthy bones and teeth, to help regulate the acid-base balance in the body, and to help regulate enzymes used in metabolism.

Magnesium is called into play for muscle contraction, in the transmission of nerve impulses, in the activation of certain enzymes, and in the proper structuring of bones and teeth.

Pantothenic acid figures in energy production, and the synthesis of fatty acids, sterols, steroid hormones, and amino acids.

You can't expect your body to function efficiently without certain vitamins and minerals, including those just discussed. As a guide to what you need, the federal government devised the RDAs, which represent what an "average" adult needs daily for good health, with a little extra thrown in for good measure. Actually, of course, there is no such thing as the "average" adult.

Some people, to function at their best, need more or less of a particular vitamin or mineral, as some people need more or less sleep. But the RDA can be used as a guideline, a fair approximation.

Some nutritionists and food faddists feel that these allowances are far too low for even the "average," and some people think them too high. But the RDAs are still a base from which to work.

As you can see, yogurt will provide you with a hefty proportion of your need for important vitamins and minerals.

This is not to say that you'll drop dead at the end of the week if you haven't been eating properly. But scientists are becoming more and more concerned with the junked-up diet of Americans.

George Briggs, for one. Briggs is a professor of nutrition at the University of California. He estimates that 30 to 40 percent of Americans who don't eat properly feel no immediate ill effects. But in twenty years—bang!—it may catch up with them. Says Briggs, "They are likely to suffer the consequences of disease unless they remedy their eating habits."

Disease such as "softening of the bones, diabetes, heart disease, or other nutritionally related disease."

For a lot of people, the end of adolescence, with Mommy no longer at your shoulder telling you what to eat, means the end of milk drinking. But they substitute no other calcium source.

Some adults cut down on milk consumption, but not voluntarily. As they get older many people—especially blacks—suffer from a deficiency of lactase, a digestive enzyme that splits milk sugar, or lactose, into the simpler glucose and galactose. Result: They cannot consume milk without discomfort.

Yogurt is a good source of calcium.

In the fermentation process, by fortuitous happenstance, lactose is already partially broken down; therefore, people with a lactase deficiency can digest yogurt even though they can't digest milk. Doctors may recommend yogurt to them as a source of calcium.

It was Elie Metchnikoff who started modern scientific investigation of yogurt.

Metchnikoff was that Russian-born biologist who won the Nobel Prize for his theory that white blood corpuscles known as phagocytes attacked and destroyed bacteria. Working at the Pasteur Institute in Paris, he turned his inquisitive attention to longevity.

Why did some people live to be 110, whereas others didn't make it to 45? It became Metchnikoff's contention that there was no planned obsolescence built into the body, that given a disease-free chance, the body could function very nicely for 150 years.

Metchnikoff set out to isolate the factors that caused premature aging.

After much research, Metchnikoff thought that the large intestine was the villain. It was there, he reasoned, that putrefying bacteria set up shop and weakened the body's systems. Having arrived at this conclusion, he couldn't do much with it, since removing everyone's large intestine didn't sound like such a great idea.

Stymied, Metchnikoff turned to statistics. He would find a population that lived a long time, study them, and figure out why they lived so long.

Plowing through the figures, Metchnikoff came up with a report showing that for every one thousand deaths recorded in Bulgaria, four were of people more than a hundred years old. This figure was far above the European average and seemed to confirm the ideas Metchnikoff had had during his earlier Bulgarian vacation.

Metchnikoff had his population; now he had to find his longevity factor.

He felt he had it when he noticed that the Bulgarian peasants were prodigious yogurt eaters, consuming as much as several quarts a day per person.

Back to the laboratory to focus his microscope.

Eureka!

Metchnikoff isolated *Lactobacillus bulgaricus* and *Streptococcus thermophilus,* and he thought he'd discovered the Fountain of Youth.

These little bacteria, he figured, were what kept those Bulgarians chugging along. These little bacteria, he decided, were what killed off the "wild and crazy" bacilli in the body and allowed the Bulgarians to grow so very old.

The theory, as nice as it sounded, did not win Metchnikoff his second Nobel Prize. Nor did it get Metchnikoff to the age he predicted he would reach,

150. Despite consuming prodigious amounts of yogurt, Metchnikoff died at 71.

Although his theory has been relegated to dusty shelves of scientific curiosities, it did serve to popularize yogurt in Europe and to suggest that further studies should be undertaken.

Recent work done by federal Department of Agriculture scientists has come up with some interesting results concerning yogurt. They found that laboratory rats fed a diet of nothing but yogurt grew 15 to 20 percent faster than rats eating buttermilk, fresh milk, or acidophilus milk—a product with a different type of bacteria than yogurt.

The experimental results led Dr. John Alford, chief of the Dairy Foods Nutrition Laboratory at the Beltsville Agricultural Research Center in Maryland, to state, "For the first time the belief that yogurt is good for you is substantiated in controlled animal studies. And that the view widely held by nutritionists that all fermented milks have a similar nutritional value was proven false.

"Why yogurt speeds growth, we don't know yet. Perhaps it is a vitamin, perhaps it is some other factor. But there is obviously something there, something good."

Referring to the Dannon Soviet Georgian TV commercials, he added, "I think total lifestyle is a more important factor in longevity than just what we eat, but I don't discount the effects of eating yogurt."

Noted nutritionist Dr. Neil Solomon, in one of his

question-and-answer columns concerning the findings of the Department of Agriculture, concluded with, "In several European and Asian countries eating yogurt has been linked to good nutrition and long life. So perhaps there is really something scientific to their century-old beliefs."

Whatever comes of future experiments, yogurt will remain a nutritionally sound part of any balanced diet. As Doctor Alford has said, "So far no one has found any reasons not to eat yogurt."

And there are certainly many reasons to eat it— including the fact that it tastes so good.

YOGURT, YOU, AND DIETING

Some people will do almost anything to lose weight.

Take Allan Carr. He's the very successful young producer of such movies as *Grease* and *Saturday Night Fever*. Carr set out on his gold-brick road to fortune by co-managing Ann-Margret's career.

Now, Allan Carr would seem to have it made. He's rich, he has a certain degree of power, and he throws "A" parties with invitation lists that would have turned Perle Mesta green.

Carr also drives a very expensive car with the license plate CAFTAN, in honor of the garment he feels most

comfortable wearing. Carr has almost two hundred caf-
tans in his closets.

Why?

Lucky, successful Allan Carr is also roly-poly Allan
Carr. But because our society is one in which you can't
be too rich or too thin, as the late Babe Paley, wife of
CBS head William Paley, once philosophized, Allan
Carr doesn't like being roly-poly.

So what does he do?

He checks himself into a hospital and has an intestinal bypass operation. After the bypass, there is less area
in the intestine to absorb food. Carr lost one hundred
pounds after his first operation. Then he returned to his
buffets and canapés and lunches in the fashionable bis-
tros and his dinners in swank restaurants. Gloppy this
and gloppy that, and Allan Carr was roly-poly again.

Back to the operating table, this time to have his jaws
wired together.

Mr. Leroy Crayton, Jr., had a different weight-loss
program, entirely self-conceived.

Leroy, much to his chagrin, was a rotund 250 pounds
when he decided enough was enough. So Leroy
marched himself into the Shaker Heights, Ohio, police
station and demanded a room in the pokey.

It was Leroy's hypothesis that two weeks in the slam-
mer would pare some blubbery inches off his forty-
three-inch waist.

"I've tried fasting for short periods of time," he told

unsympathetic police officers, "but I have always given in to the temptation of food."

If temptation was the problem, Leroy figured that jail food wouldn't offer any. He would have to lose weight.

Unfortunately for him, the municipal judge took exception to transforming the Shaker Heights jail into a La Costa–Midwest fat farm.

Leroy was sent home, as fat and as unhappy as ever.

Americans, it seems, have an insatiable appetite for any and all weight-reducing programs, no matter how wild, drastic, or absurd. Anything sells, as long as it comes with glowing testimonials, Before and After pictures, and promises of YOU TOO CAN LOSE WEIGHT!

We are always looking for that easy something which will eliminate all pain, suffering, and work from losing weight. If someone says that a daily shot of a pregnant woman's urine will help you lose weight, the believers will line up each day for the injection. Fat people are not necessarily more gullible than thin ones, but they are often insecure about their ability to lose weight without some miraculous crutch.

So first we present the bad news for dieters—a short examination of these crutches and whether they work.

Crutches like pills. Pop one a day and watch the fat drip away.

Pills have been popular for years, running the gamut from those sold in "beauty parlor" magazines to ones prescribed and monitored by doctors.

Ads for the former call out enticingly that "you can look like this" by merely mailing in $6.95. The pounds, say the ads, are guaranteed to disappear.

There are any number of these types of pills, and new ones appear as others are yanked off the market. One was something called Anapax, a little wonder you could have bought in 1970.

The Anapax Diet Plan Tablets pledged a loss of "85 pounds of ugly fat in only two short months." What's more, the brochure proclaimed that "doctors, nurses, actors, and models" all got rid of extra adipose with "no effort at all for the first time in their lives."

It sounded wonderful to thousands of people, but not to the attorney general of New York State. He thought the claims were basic hooey and forced the Anapax people to refund the purchase price to those who requested refunds.

Most of these pills are good for nothing more than a very temporary—and very small—dip on the scale. Anapax had a bulk producer, supposedly to eliminate hunger pangs, and another ingredient to coat the stomach's lining and suppress appetite. However, the only way to take off pounds with the Anapax diet plan tablets was to follow the Anapax low-carbohydrate *diet* that was included with the pills.

Despite what purchasers want to believe, pills in and of themselves won't make fat disappear. Changing your caloric intake will.

It's the same story with doctor-prescribed pills, most of which have an amphetamine base. To some degree amphetamines "speed" up your metabolism (hence the street name for them), but for the most part they serve as an appetite suppressant.

Dr. Jean Mayer, one of the nation's most widely known nutritionists, points out that anorexigenic agents—amephetimine derivatives—will cause a temporary weight drop, but long-term use leads to psychological dependency.

The American Medical Association has also taken a dim view of amphetamines: "Their undesirable effects, including a tendency to produce psychic and, occasionally, physical dependence when used indiscriminately and in large doses, make their use hazardous."

Dr. George V. Mann, an associate professor of biochemistry and medicine at Vanderbilt University and a career investigator for the National Heart and Lung Institute, once complained that "doctors use amphetamines as an escape mechanism to get obese patients off their backs. And they don't work. But it's much easier and much more profitable to give somebody a pill than it is to sit down and spend some time discussing alternative solutions."

Another type of pill is the diuretic, or water pill. It causes water loss, not fat loss. Except for a psychological boost—hey, gee, I'm making progress on the scale—diuretics won't accomplish what you want at all. If you lose weight only by losing water, you'll soon gain it back.

It would seem then that no matter how you look for another means, you're going to have to diet.

Which brings us to the scads of "miracle" diets that are forever surfacing. There is no shortage of diets around, from the sane to the exotic, and many have great-sounding, gimmicky names.

The Prudent Diet. The Diet Revolution. The Drinking Man's Diet. Fasting: The Ultimate Diet. The Save Your Life Diet. Dr. Solomon's Easy, No-risk Diet. The Nibbler's Diet. Yes, and even the Ice Cream Diet.

No matter what your dietary proclivities and weaknesses are, somebody has come up with what sounds like the very regimen for you.

Some of the most enticing-sounding programs are those which claim you can eat all you want of a particular food. You have a weakness for ice cream? Eat gallons. Sounds too good to be true, and it is. Although a diet's proponents may proffer wonderfully complicated reasons why this or that in their regimen causes fat to fall off, it's been found that people actually tire of eating "all they want" of one food. When they do, they unconsciously eat less. Basically, these diets work—to the extent that they do—because you eat less and therefore take in fewer calories.

The drawback to many of these programs is that they don't provide a balanced meal plan, including adequate amounts of the four basic food groups—milk, meat, vegetable-fruit, and bread-cereal. In other words, these are not nutritionally adequate programs you can live with for the rest of your life.

Furthermore, radical diets *can* be dangerous, even if you stay on them for only a couple of weeks.

As for surgical procedures, speaking of radical, even they are based on limiting calories. They have to be, because calories—which are nothing more than a measure of energy, how much energy it takes for the body to burn off food—are what fat and obesity are all about.

Besides the intestinal bypass and jaw wiring, there is now stomach stapling. It works pretty much on the same principle as intestinal bypass. Here, large stainless-steel staples close off most of the stomach, again leaving less surface to absorb food. It's supposed to produce an average loss of fifteen pounds a month.

Although surgery is drastic, so is extreme obesity. Wanting to unblubber yourself is more than a vanity; it is a necessity.

People who are one hundred, two hundred, and more pounds overweight don't need to lose only because they look grotesque, can't find clothes that fit them, and are ashamed to go to the movies because they slop over into three seats. They need to lose because they are in serious medical trouble.

Obesity can cut short your life.

It is believed that obesity contributes to diabetes, hypertension (which may lead to stroke, heart failure, and kidney malfunction), arterial disease, and more.

Furthermore, it's not always clear how much obesity contributes to other life-shortening diseases. As C. F. Gastineau, M.D., has said, "The relation between obesity and a given disease, if it exists, may not be linear; and because of practical difficulties in measuring degrees of obesity and excluding other risk factors, the hazards of being obese may not be readily proved.

"Some hazards are clear."

What if you're not obese, but merely overweight? It's still not vanity to shed pounds, as statistics show.

A study by the Society of Actuaries found, among other things, that the mortality rate for men between fifteen and sixty-nine years old was one-third greater for those who were 20 percent and more overweight. Being only 10 percent overweight increased the mortality rate by one-fifth.

The United States Senate staff of the Select Committee on Nutrition and Human Needs estimates that being 10 percent overweight is as hazardous to your health as smoking *twenty* cigarettes a day.

Now if those figures aren't enough to make you want to slim down, social scientists are finding that "ugly" people—and fatties are thrown into that category—have to deal with a society that has a strong bias against them.

Teachers think good-looking kids are brighter than ugly ones.

Jurors are more likely to believe an attractive witness or defendant than an unattractive one.

Ugly mental patients are often given more severe diagnoses and are hospitalized longer.

Homely people get paid less. (Talk about fighting the ugly bias to the federal Equal Employment Opportunity Commission, and the response is, "Ha, ha!")

Physical appearance affects who wins public office.

As Dorothy Lynch of the Cambridge Research Associates sees it, "It is a visceral thing. People don't usually say in polls that they find a candidate physically repulsive, but it sometimes shows up in other measures."

In 1973 it showed up when her group was polling for a then very fat Maynard Jackson, who was running for the mayor's office in Atlanta.

"We got indications that people thought he wasn't very self-disciplined, that he was too expansive and jolly. Well, Jackson was about 150 pounds overweight then. We recommended he lose a lot of weight. He did and those objection factors disappeared."

Where does all this leave the overweight and obese? It leaves them needing to lose weight.

The first thing to remember is that with a very few exceptions—and in all likelihood you aren't one of them—you *can* lose weight.

The way to do it is not with some super-duper, eat-only-yogurt diet, either. Sure, it would be nice to tell you that strawberry yogurt has magical properties whereby *Lactobacillus bulgaricus* goes crazy eating your fat cells. Like to be able to tell you that, but it's not true.

(A New York doctor once told of a patient who came in complaining there was something wrong with him. The patient couldn't lose weight. When questioned it turned out that the man was still eating everything he had always eaten, but he had *added* five containers of yogurt a day to his diet.

("I thought eating yogurt was supposed to make you lose weight," he explained.)

Once you realize that you can lose weight, despite all your previous experiences, *you can keep it off too.*

There is little good in turning yourself into a human yo-yo—fat to thin, thin to fat. It's not healthy. And that's an inherent fault with most diets. They have short-term effect. You might lose weight, but the loss is temporary. What you need to do is lose weight for a lifetime.

How can you make this miracle of miracles occur?

Simple.

By changing your eating habits.

By changing your attitudes and conceptions of food.

By starting now.

You don't have to be fat. You're the one making you fat. If you can make yourself fat, then you can make yourself thin.

No kidding.

So where does yogurt come in, since its bacteria aren't newly discovered, fat-hating wonder organisms?

Yogurt can be an integral part of a workable, enjoyable, and delicious eating plan that will take you from tubby to trim, and keep you there.

For those who like—or need—specific, follow-this-meal-by-meal guidance, a sensible, tasty, and filling diet follows.

But first, a general discussion about you and food.

To a lot of pudgies, eating is a bad habit.

You start the day off with a breakfast of presugared cereal and a couple of pieces of toast with jam. You grab a candy bar on your way to work. Then it's a cupcake at coffee break. A ham-and-cheese sandwich for lunch. Peanuts in the afternoon, washed down by a soda or two. Some potato chips to stave off starvation before dinner.

And then you're ready for serious eating. Starches, sugars, calorie-laden meat, topped off by pie à la mode. But you're not finished. There is still time for an orgy of munchies while you watch television.

All this food tallies up to a horrendous four-thousand-plus calories in a single day.

Horrendous? Sure, when you realize that thirty-five hundred extra calories equal an extra pound.

For example's sake, let's say your are a five-foot, five-inch woman. Your weight is fairly normal, 120 pounds or so. You're not totally sedentary but not very active either. These are rough figures, but depending on your age and frame, you need approximately fifteen hundred to two thousand calories a day to maintain your weight.

If, however, you start force feeding yourself that incredible diet of four thousand calories a day, simple arithmetic shows what will happen. You're going to gain weight.

It doesn't matter if you swear up and down the kitchen that you eat like a bird. Your body's calorie calculator will not be fooled. If you put more calories in than you use, there will be an excess. The body stores excess. It stores excess in the form of fat.

Make up your mind to stop this nonsense. But first, you're going to have to pinpoint the nonsense.

That's your first assignment.

You may think you know what your eating problems are, but don't be too sure.

STEP NUMBER ONE: Start a food diary.
Every time you eat, note the following items:

1. The actual time you start to eat and the actual time you finish.

2. Where you eat.

3. The position you eat in—sitting, standing, lying down.

4. Whether you are alone or with others when you eat.

5. Whether you do anything else, such as reading or watching television, while you eat.

6. How hungry you are, if at all, when you begin eating. Rate this on a scale of one to ten, with ten being ravenous.

7. What your mood is when you eat—happy, sad, ready to kick the world in the pants.

8. What you eat and in what quantity.

Put this in chart form. And don't cheat. Don't wait until evening to say, "Let's see, what was it I had for lunch?" *Every time* food, snacks, or liquids with calories go into your mouth, write it down immediately. (Unsweetened coffee and tea don't count. Neither does water.)

The diary will serve two purposes.

One, you will stop eating absentmindedly. "Tastes" while you're cooking or licks of someone else's ice-cream cone get added on your calorie calculator, as does a five-course meal for which you made reservations at Maxim's five months ago.

Two, the diary will start to show patterns.

You may find that although you eat perfectly sensibly and within reasonable caloric boundaries from breakfast to dinner, while you're watching Charlie's Angels do in another no-goodnik you start stuffing yourself. Or you might find that you overeat when you are unhappy or tense or angry. You might be a solitary overindulger, someone who doesn't eat enough to keep a canary going when you're with someone but gourmandizes enough to keep King Kong filled when you're alone.

Figure it out. Watch your pattern.

And then do something about it.

STEP NUMBER TWO: Don't be afraid to play mind games with yourself.

As has been noted, gluttony is a habit, a bad habit. It probably took you years to develop it and to get firmly entrenched in it. Exchange your bad eating habits for good ones. It *can* be done, despite the reasons you began overeating—whether it was Mommy ordering you to clean your plate because of poor, starving orphans in China or because you are bored and frustrated.

Mind games can be useful for everyone and anyone. One seems to help opera star Luciano Pavarotti.

Pavarotti lost ninety pounds in eighteen months by

holding to a sensible and satisfying eighteen-hundred-calorie-a-day diet. (He travels with two scales—one for himself and one for his food.)

But everyone needs a change of pace now and then, even Pavarotti. When he does, he plays a trick on himself.

Wrote Stephen E. Rubin in the *New York Times Magazine*, "Pavarotti sometimes departs from his regimen. He graciously pours what he dubs 'tentative Irish coffee' (made with J&B Scotch) into tacky mugs, after downing a half pint of what he persists in calling 'ice cream, so light and delicate' even though the container plainly says, 'Dannon Frozen Lowfat Vanilla Yogurt.' "

Eating frozen yogurt instead of ice cream for dessert is one diet trick, but here are more general tips in modifying your eating behavior.

1. When you're eating, that should be the only thing you do. No reading. No crossword puzzles. No *Gong Show.*

2. Eat sitting down. Don't eat standing up or lying down. Otherwise, when you open the refrigerator door you forget and start taking a nibble of whatever is in sight.

3. Put the food you like out of sight, at the back of the refrigerator or pantry.

4. Keep your eating contained to one room or two. That way eating will become associated with the dining

room or kitchen. After a while the cue to eat in other rooms will begin to disappear.

5. Make a happy production out of your meal. Set the table properly. Make eating an occasion. Bring out the candles. Make eating a pleasure-filled experience that you enjoy for its own sake.

6. Serve yourself from the kitchen. Don't keep serving dishes and platters on the table. That makes taking seconds a more conscious decision. If you want more, you're going to have to get up and move for it—which means a little extra time to ask yourself whether you really want that additional food. After all, the pleasure of eating lasts a few minutes. You have to carry the extra weight around with you twenty-four hours a day.

7. Be aware of your mood before you sit down. Ask yourself, "What are my emotions now? How do I feel?" Awareness is the first step in controlling your emotions and your eating. After all, if you're mad at your mate, overeating isn't going to harm him or her. You're the victim.

8. Don't start bolting your food as soon as you sit down. Wait a minute or two. A meal isn't an Olympic event.

9. Eat slowly. Many overeaters are fast eaters. Savor your food. You might even close your eyes once in a while and say, "Taste and texture." It may have been years since you've actually tasted what you've eaten.

10. Put your fork down between bites. It's a matter of being self-conscious, of not indulging in mindless eating.

11. Don't refill your fork until you've finished chewing and swallowing.

12. And you know, despite what Mommy told you, you don't *have* to finish everything on your plate. Try pushing a few bites aside at the beginning of the meal and having them still be there at the end. Demonstrate your control.

13. When you're finished eating, either remove your plate from the table and return if not everyone else has finished, or totally remove yourself from the dining area. No point in overtempting yourself. If at the end of the meal you still feel "hungry," don't immediately load up your plate. Wait fifteen minutes: It may take a while before your brain catches up with your stomach. It may be that you're actually full but your satiety mechanism hasn't had time to react.

You don't have to master all these "behavior modification" techniques at once. Start with one or two. Set goals, realistic goals. Make the techniques part of your eating routine. Make them habit.

Another facet of eating awareness is calorie awareness.

Test yourself. How many calories are there in one tablespoon of peanut butter? Eighty-two. Now think of how much you ordinarily spread onto a couple of

CALORIE DIARY

	FIRST DAY	SECOND DAY	THIRD DAY
BREAKFAST			
MIDMORNING			
LUNCH			
AFTERNOON			
SUPPER			
EVENING			

71

pieces of bread and top off with a glob of jelly, if you are a peanut-butter-and-jelly-sandwich fan. You're talking about nearly five hundred calories.

Get thee to a bookshop and buy thee a complete calorie counter. A less extensive one appears at the end of this chapter.

There are two ways to keep track of your calorie consumption.

One is to keep a running total of calories consumed until you have reached your daily limit. The other way is to start with the calories you are allowed for the day and then subtract as you eat something. This is the "savings withdrawal" technique. Whichever way you do it, keep within your caloric limit. Make it easy for yourself. Set up a calorie diary like the one that appears on page 71.

Calorie counting is more than simply a "numbers game." Eating twelve hundred calories' worth of chocolate bars a day is not what calorie counting is all about. Calories have to be spaced and divided over foods that fulfill your body's nutritional needs.

Face it. If your body is going to function properly, you have to tank up with the right fuel. Pump olive oil into your Ford or Mercedes instead of gasoline, and you can expect the car to stall out, or worse.

Your daily calorie quota must be filled with the right kind of calories, not empty ones. This doesn't mean cutting out snacks, either. Snacks can pick you up and increase your energy. For some people with a tendency to have the afternoon blahs because of lowered blood sugar, snacks are a real necessity.

The trick to snacking is what you choose to eat between meals. Forget those peanut and potato-chip breaks. Try yogurt instead. It supplies protein and nutrients essential to your health. Some yogurts, such as Dannon, remove about half the butterfat so they are 98 to 99 percent fat free. *And* a cup of yogurt is satisfying. It will keep those hunger pangs away. When it comes time to sit down for a full meal, you won't gorge because you feel you're on the verge of starvation.

If you really want to be calorie stingy, zip up a cup of plain yogurt (150 calories) even further by adding any of the following. Suggested by Willetta Warberg, a leading food consultant, these additions increase the calorie count by only about twenty-five calories.

Stir in:

 2 teaspoons frozen fruit-juice concentrate
   (orange, lemon-lime, pineapple, etc.)
 1 teaspoon sweetened soft-drink mix
 1 teaspoon flavored gelatin-dessert powder
 1 teaspoon instant cocoa or carob powder
 1 teaspoon pudding mix
 1 teaspoon instant presweetened tea
 1 teaspoon maple syrup
 1 teaspoon sugar and a dash of fresh lemon or
   lime juice
 1 teaspoon chocolate syrup
 1 tablespoon applesauce and a dash of cinnamon

1 tablespoon sweetened coconut flakes
1 teaspoon dietetic preserves or marmalade
1 tablespoon canned nectar (pear, peach, apricot, etc.)
1 tablespoon liqueur (Curaçao or crème de menthe or de cacao)
1 teaspoon instant onion soup mix or other soup mix
1 packet instant vegetable-broth mix
1 tablespoon relish (frankfurter or hamburger)
1 teaspoon tartar sauce
1 teaspoon each catsup and brown sugar
½ teaspoon each prepared mustard and sugar
1 tablespoon each canned minced clams and dried chopped chives
1 tablespoon canned deviled ham
1 tablespoon mashed canned tuna fish
2 tablespoons cottage cheese
1 teaspoon each grated parmesan or romano cheese and catsup

To get you started losing weight, try the Dannon seven-day diet plan. There are actually two, one for nine hundred to a thousand calories a day, the other for fifteen hundred to sixteen hundred. You might try one week at the lower calorie level and the next week at the higher.

Although this is a perfectly sound diet developed by Willetta Warberg and approved by Dr. Rose Mirenda, talk it over with your doctor. In fact, talk over any diet with your doctor, unless you plan to cut down by only a few calories per day.

Don't expect or want to lose all your extra fat at once. It took you a while to put it on; it will take you a while to take it off.

Also remember that increasing the amount you exercise, be it ever so minimal, will increase the amount of energy your body uses up. When you reduce your food intake and increase your energy output, your weight-reduction program—and the speed with which you lose—will benefit. But don't expect to go out and run off all extra weight in an hour. It takes one minute of walking to expend five or six calories. One minute of swimming for eleven calories, nineteen calories for a minute of running.

Take a look at this exercise equivalency chart from the American Heart Association and the Nutrition Foundation to acquaint yourself with some common exercise expenditures.

EXERCISE-ACTIVITY TABLE

	Calories Per Hour		Calories Per Hour
bicycling	300–420	Ping-Pong	360
bowling	260	running	800–1,000
dancing	450–700	skating	300–700
gardening	350	skiing	600
golf	210–300	swimming	350–700
housework	180–240	tennis	400–500
horseback riding	180–480	volleyball	210
ice skating	360	walking	100–330

75

Exercising isn't only jogging and calisthenics. Make it part of your daily activities to bend, reach, and walk more. Don't drive around for ten minutes looking for the parking spot closest to the supermarket. Leave your car at the end of the lot. Hike it. Take stairs instead of elevators. Leave the car at home if your destination is within walking distance. Don't ask Junior to fetch the telephone book. Get it yourself. Stand up when making a telephone call or dictating to your secretary. (But don't stand up while you're eating.) Find other ways, small and large, to increase your physical activity—*and* set up a weekly program of more strenuous workouts. Try jogging or jumping rope. You're going to feel better.

And try the Dannon Seven-Day Diet Plan. A major consumer-health publication recently rated it among the top reducing diets. You'll like it.

MONDAY

900 to 1000 Calories	1500 to 1600 Calories

Breakfast

½ grapefruit	½ grapefruit
1 container plain yogurt	1 container coffee, lemon, or
1 slice whole-wheat toast	vanilla yogurt
small pat butter or margarine	1 slice whole-wheat toast
plain coffee or tea	small pat butter or margarine
	plain coffee or tea

Midmorning snack

4 dried apricot halves	4 dried apricot halves

Lunch

small glass tomato juice	small glass tomato juice
¼ cup scoop tuna-fish salad	⅓ cup scoop tuna-fish-salad
on lettuce	sandwich on whole-wheat bread
1 slice whole-wheat toast	plain coffee or tea
plain coffee or tea	

Midafternoon snack

container plain, coffee, lemon, or	1 container fruit yogurt
vanilla yogurt	

Dinner

3-ounce slice beef liver sautéed in	4-ounce slice beef liver sautéed in
small pat butter or margarine	small pat butter or margarine
8 spears cooked asparagus	8 spears cooked asparagus
½ medium-size baked potato	½ medium-sized baked potato
small tossed green salad with	small tossed green salad with
lemon juice	lemon juice
plain coffee or tea	plain coffee or tea

Bedtime snack

1 glass skim milk	1 container fruit yogurt

TUESDAY

900 to 1000 Calories	1500 to 1600 Calories

Breakfast

½ cantaloupe	½ cantaloupe
1 container plain yogurt	1 container coffee, lemon, or vanilla
1 slice whole-wheat toast	yogurt
small pat butter or margarine	1 slice whole-wheat toast
plain coffee or tea	small pat butter or margarine
	plain coffee or tea

Midmorning snack

| 4 dried "softenized" prunes | 4 dried "softenized" prunes |

Lunch

1-ounce slice cheese, lettuce, and	1 cup vegetable beef soup
tomato sandwich on whole-wheat	1-ounce slice cheese, lettuce, and
bread, *no mayonnaise*	tomato sandwich on whole-wheat
plain coffee or tea	bread, *no mayonnaise*
	plain coffee or tea

Midafternoon snack

| 1 container plain, coffee, lemon, | 1 container fruit yogurt |
| or vanilla yogurt | |

Dinner

1½-ounce lean slice roast pork	2 1½-ounce lean slices roast pork
7 or 8 cooked brussels sprouts	7 or 8 cooked brussels sprouts
¼ cup unsweetened applesauce	¼ cup unsweetened applesauce
plain coffee or tea	½ small baked sweet potato
	plain coffee or tea

Bedtime snack

| 1 glass skim milk | 1 container fruit yogurt |

78

WEDNESDAY

900 to 1000 Calories	1500 to 1600 Calories

Breakfast

small glass prune juice	small glass prune juice
1 container plain yogurt	1 container coffee, lemon, or
1 slice whole-wheat toast	vanilla yogurt
small pat butter or margarine	1 slice whole-wheat toast
plain coffee or tea	small pat butter or margarine
	plain coffee or tea

Midmorning snack

4 dried apricot halves	4 dried apricot halves

Lunch

4 canned sardines (1½ ounces,	1 cup beef broth, bouillon, or
drained of oil)	consommé
½ hard-cooked egg	4 canned sardines (1½ ounces,
wedge of lettuce	drained of oil)
1 sliced tomato	1 hard-cooked egg
1 slice whole-wheat toast	wedge of lettuce
plain coffee or tea	1 sliced tomato
	1 slice whole-wheat toast
	plain coffee or tea

Midafternoon snack

1 container plain, coffee, lemon, or	1 container fruit yogurt
vanilla yogurt	

Dinner

3 slices baked, broiled, or stewed	¼ small baked, broiled, or stewed
breast of chicken plus the liver	breast of chicken plus the liver
½ cup cooked spinach	½ cup cooked spinach
¼ cup ready-to-serve instant rice	½ cup ready-to-serve instant rice
plain coffee or tea	plain coffee or tea

Bedtime snack

1 glass skim milk	1 container fruit yogurt

THURSDAY

900 to 1000 Calories   1500 to 1600 Calories

Breakfast

½ cantaloupe
1 container plain yogurt
1 slice whole-wheat toast
small pat butter or margarine
plain coffee or tea

½ cantaloupe
1 container coffee, lemon, or vanilla yogurt
1 slice whole-wheat toast
small pat butter or margarine
plain coffee or tea

Midmorning snack

1 small box raisins (1½ Tbs per pkg.)

1 small box raisins (1½ Tbs per pkg.)

Lunch

⅓-cup scoop chopped chicken liver on lettuce
1 sliced tomato
2 rye wafers
plain coffee or tea

⅓-cup scoop chopped chicken liver on lettuce
1 sliced tomato
4 rye wafers
½ cup fresh fruit salad
plain coffee or tea

Midafternoon snack

1 container plain, coffee, lemon, or vanilla yogurt

1 container fruit yogurt

Dinner

3-ounce grilled minute steak
½ cup cooked carrots
½ cup cooked broccoli
½ medium-sized baked potato
plain coffee or tea

4-ounce grilled minute steak
½ cup cooked carrots
½ cup cooked broccoli
½ medium-size baked potato
plain coffee or tea

Bedtime snack

1 glass skim milk

1 container fruit yogurt

FRIDAY

900 to 1000 Calories   1500 to 1600 Calories

Breakfast
small glass orange juice
1 container plain yogurt
1 slice whole-wheat toast
small pat butter or margarine
plain coffee or tea

small glass orange juice
1 container coffee, lemon, or
vanilla yogurt
1 slice whole-wheat toast
small pat butter or margarine
plain coffee or tea

Midmorning snack
4 dried apricot halves   4 dried apricot halves

Lunch
2 poached or hard-cooked eggs
1 slice whole-wheat toast
small tossed green salad with
lemon juice
plain coffee or tea

small glass tomato juice
2 poached or hard-cooked eggs
2 slices whole-wheat toast
small tossed green salad with
lemon juice
plain coffee or tea

Midafternoon snack
1 container plain, coffee, lemon, or
vanilla yogurt

1 container fruit yogurt

Dinner
3-ounce swordfish steak broiled with
small pat butter or margarine
½ cup cooked spinach
½ cup cooked cauliflower
½ small soft roll
plain coffee or tea

1 cup clam chowder
3-ounce swordfish steak broiled
with small pat butter or margarine
½ cup cooked spinach
½ cup cooked cauliflower
½ small soft roll
plain coffee or tea

Bedtime snack
1 glass skim milk   1 container fruit yogurt

81

SATURDAY

900 to 1000 Calories	1500 to 1600 Calories

Breakfast

½ grapefruit
1 container plain yogurt
1 slice whole-wheat toast
small pat butter or margarine
plain coffee or tea

½ grapefruit
1 container coffee, lemon, or vanilla yogurt
1 slice whole-wheat toast
small pat butter or margarine
plain coffee or tea

Midmorning snack

1 small box raisins (1½ Tbs per pkg.)

1 small box raisins (1½ Tbs per pkg.)

Lunch

3-ounce hamburger patty
1 slice whole-wheat bread
½ cup cooked carrots
plain coffee or tea

1 cup beef broth, bouillon, or consommé
cheeseburger made with 3-ounce hamburger patty, 1-ounce slice cheese
½ cup cooked carrots
plain coffee or tea

Midafternoon snack

1 container plain, coffee, lemon, or vanilla yogurt

1 container fruit yogurt

Dinner

3 1-ounce breaded fish sticks
1 Tbs catsup
½ cup cooked green beans
¼ cup ready-to-serve instant rice
plain coffee or tea

6 1-ounce breaded fish sticks
2 Tbs catsup
½ cup cooked green beans
¼ cup ready-to-serve instant rice
plain coffee or tea

Bedtime snack

1 glass skim milk

1 container fruit yogurt

82

SUNDAY

900 to 1000 Calories	1500 to 1600 Calories

Breakfast

small glass orange juice	small glass orange juice
1 container plain yogurt	1 container coffee, lemon, or
1 slice whole-wheat toast	vanilla yogurt
small pat butter or margarine	1 slice whole-wheat toast
plain coffee or tea	small pat butter or margarine
	plain coffee or tea

Midmorning snack

4 dried "softenized" prunes	4 dried "softenized" prunes

Lunch

1 small canned salmon steak	small glass tomato juice
1 slice whole-wheat toast	1 small canned salmon steak
1 fresh carrot	1 slice whole-wheat toast
celery sticks and radish roses	1 fresh carrot
plain coffee or tea	celery sticks and radish roses
	plain coffee or tea

Midafternoon snack

1 container plain, coffee, lemon, or vanilla yogurt	1 container fruit yogurt

Dinner

1 2½-ounce lean slice pot roast	1 cup vegetable soup
1 small boiled potato	2 2½-ounce lean slices pot roast
½ cup cooked green peas	1 small boiled potato
plain coffee or tea	½ cup cooked green peas
	plain coffee or tea

Bedtime snack

1 glass skim milk	1 container fruit yogurt

CALORIE GUIDE TO
COMMON FOODS

BEVERAGES

	Approx. Calories		Approx. Calories
Alcoholic:		Cocoa, homemade, with	
Beer, 12 ounces	150	whole milk	245
Brandy, 1½ ounces		Cocoa, instant, made	
(80 proof)	100	with water	100
Champagne, 3½ ounces			
(dry)	74	**Coffee, 1 cup:**	
Cordials, 1 ounce		Black, no sugar	5
(average proof)	97	Black, 1 tsp. sugar	20
Gin, 1½ ounces		Regular, 1 Tbs milk,	
(94 proof)	115	1 tsp sugar	30
Rum, 1½ ounces			
(94 proof)	115	**Fruit drink, 8 ounces:**	
Vodka, 1½ ounces		All fruit drinks	100 to 130
(94 proof)	115		
Whiskey, 1½ ounces		**Fruit juice, 8 ounces:**	
(94 proof)	115	Apple	120
Wine, 3½ ounces		Cranberry cocktail	147
Table: chablis,		Grape	165
claret, etc.	85	Grapefruit, fresh	95
Dessert: muscatel,		Grapefruit, canned,	
port, etc.	140	unsweetened	100
		Orange, fresh	110
		Orange, canned	
Carbonated, nonalcoholic,		unsweetened	120
sweetened, 12 ounces:		Pineapple, canned	135
Cola	145	Prune	200
Diet and low calorie	1 to 8	Tomato	45
Fruit-flavored	170		
Ginger ale	115	**Milk, 8 ounces:**	
Plain	115	Buttermilk, 1% fat	90
		Nonfat, reconstituted	
		skim	80
Chocolate or Cocoa, 1 cup		Skim, fortified	90
hot or cold:		Whole	160
Chocolate-flavored drink		1%	110
with skim milk	190	Chocolate milk shake	421
		Ice-cream soda	230
		Malted Milk	245

	Approx. Calories		Approx. Calories
Tea, 1 cup:		**Toasts, 1 slice:**	
Plain	2	Holland rusk	50
With lemon	4	Melba, white	15
With lemon and 1 tsp		Zwieback	31
sugar	19		
With 1 Tbs milk, 1 tsp			
sugar	27	**CEREALS**	

Dry, ready to eat, 1 cup:

BREADS, BISCUITS, MUFFINS, ROLLS		All bran	190
		Bran flakes, plain	105
		Bran flakes with	
Breads, 1 slice:		raisins	145
Boston brown	100	Corn flakes, plain	100
Cracked or whole		Corn flakes, sugared	155
wheat	65	Grape Nuts	440
French	58	Puffed oats	100
Italian	55	Puffed rice	60
Protein	45	Puffed wheat	55
Rye	60	Puffed wheat, sugared	130
White	65 to 70	Rice flakes	123
		Shredded wheat,	
		1 large biscuit	90
Biscuits, baking powder:		Wheat flakes	104
1 biscuit, 2-inch		Wheat germ, 1 Tbs	36
diameter	90 to 105		

Muffins:		**Cooked, 1 cup:**	
Bran	113	Cream of wheat	
Corn	130	(quick)	130
English	135	Farina	105
		Oatmeal	130
Rolls:		Wheat, cracked	138
Bagel	165		
Frankfurter	120		
Hard	155		

85

	Approx. Calories		Approx. Calories

CRACKERS AND SNACKS, 1 piece:

Butter thin	18
Cheese/peanut butter	39
Cheese tidbit	2
Hi-Ho, Ritz	17
Matzo	78
Onion	11
Oyster	3
Popcorn, 1 cup with oil and salt	40
Popcorn, 1 cup, sugar coated	135
Potato chip, 1 large	11
Pretzel, Dutch, large twisted	60
Pretzel stick, 2¼ inches long and thin	1
Rye Krisp	21
Saltine	12
Triscuit	21
Wheat Thin	9

DAIRY PRODUCTS (See beverages for milk and milk drinks)

Cheeses, 1 ounce:

American, blue, Roquefort, Swiss	105
Camembert	86
Cheddar	115
Cottage, creamed	30
Cottage, uncreamed	24
Cream	106
Edam	87
Gruyere	115

Cheese spreads, 1 ounce:

| Velveeta | 80 |

Creams, 1 ounce:

Creamer, powdered, nondairy, 1 level tsp	10
Light, 18% fat	63
Half and half, 12% fat	40
Heavy	105
Whipping, light, unwhipped	89
Whipped topping, pressurized, 1 Tbs	10
Sour	60

Milk desserts, ½ cup:

| Custard, baked | 152 |
| Sherbet | 130 |

Ice creams:

All flavors, 1 large scoop	150 to 250
Chocolate-covered bar	162
Sandwich	208

Cones:

| Sugar cone | 45 |
| Waffle cone | 19 |

Ice milks:

| All flavors, 1 large scoop | 100 to 150 |
| Chocolate-covered bar | 144 |

	Approx. Calories		Approx. Calories
Yogurts:		Egg salad	335
Dannon, plain	150	Frankfurter	290
Dannon, coffee, vanilla,		Grilled cheese	380
lemon	200	Ham, boiled	262
Dannon, fruit	260	Ham and cheese	296
Danny Frozen-		Hamburger	305
yogurt bar	120	Liverwurst	310
Danny-Yo soft frozen		Meat loaf	301
yogurt, 3		Peanut butter, lettuce	304
ounces weight	100	Peanut butter, and	
		jelly	344
		Roast beef	375
EGGS, 1 medium		Salmon, smoked, with	
Hard or soft cooked,		cream cheese,	
poached	80	on bagel	321
Fried with 1 tsp fat	123	Steak, sliced	260
Omelet made with 1		Tuna salad	225
tsp fat, 1 Tbs milk	128	**SAUCES, 1 Tbs**	
		Barbecue catsup, chili	15
FATS AND OILS,		Gravy	40 to 90
1 Tbs		Hollandaise	48
Butter, margarine	100	Soy, Worcestershire	12
Lard	115	Tartar	76
Oil (corn, olive,		**SOUPS, canned, 1 cup**	
peanut, safflower,		Bean with pork	170
salad)	125	Beef broth	30
		Beef noodle	70
		Beef vegetable	80
SANDWICHES		Chicken noodle	58
Bacon, lettuce,		Chicken with rice	37
tomato	270	Chicken gumbo	94
Chicken salad	322	Clam chowder	80
Chicken, sliced	217	Cream of asparagus	101
Cheese, sliced tomato		Cream of mushroom	215
and lettuce	280	Minestrone	105
Cheeseburger	410	Onion	59
Chopped chicken		Pea	145
livers	272	Tomato prepared	
Club	412	with water	90

	Approx. Calories			Approx. Calories

FISH AND SHELLFISH, 4 ounces

Bluefish, broiled	133
Clams, raw	87
Clams, canned	60
Codfish, broiled	194
Crab, canned	113
Crab, soft shell, fried	185
Fish sticks, breaded	200
Flounder, broiled	205
Haddock, fried	189
Halibut, broiled	195
Herring, kippered, smoked	241
Lobster, broiled	103
Mackerel, broiled	270
Mackerel, smoked	248
Oysters, raw	75
Oysters, fried	273
Perch, fried	260
Salmon, broiled	208
Salmon, canned	230
Salmon, smoked	201
Sardines, canned, drained	232
Sardines with tomato sauce	224
Scallops, broiled	91
Scallops, breaded	222
Shrimp, boiled or broiled	103
Shrimp, breaded	158
Shrimp, canned, drained	84
Tuna, canned, drained	190

MEATS

Beef, 3-ounce serving:

Braised	245
Corned, boiled	318
Corned, plain, canned	157
Corned, hash, canned	154
Hamburger, lean round, broiled	185
Liver, fried	196
Meat loaf	171
Pot roast	245
Roast rib, lean meat only	206
Steak, T-bone, sirloin, and porterhouse, lean meat only, broiled	191
Steak, boneless chuck, lean meat only, broiled	188
Steak, boneless round, lean meat only, broiled	162

Lamb, 3-ounce serving:

Chop, lean meat only, broiled	177
Leg, lean meat only, roasted	159

Pork, 3-ounce serving:

Chop, lean meat only, broiled	229
Ham, cured, lean meat only, cooked	245
Roast loin, lean meat only	218

	Approx. Calories
Veal, 3-ounce serving:	
Cutlet, boneless, broiled	185
Liver, calf's, fried	224
Stew with vegetables, ½ cup	121
Poultry, 3-ounce serving:	
Chicken:	
Broiled, meat only	115
Canned, meat only	170
Fried, ½ breast	155
Fried, drumstick	129
Liver, broiled	141
Pie with vegetables	201
Duck:	
Roasted, meat only	227
Turkey:	
Canned, meat only	173
Roasted, dark meat only	174
Roasted, light meat only	151

MEAT PRODUCTS

Bacon, 1 slice, broiled	45
Bologna, 1 ounce	86
Frankfurter, boiled or broiled	170
Ham, boiled, 1 ounce	66
Ham, minced, canned, 1 ounce	65
Liverwurst, 1 ounce	90
Pork sausage, cooked, 1 ounce	63
Salami, 1 ounce	88

	Approx. Calories
TV DINNERS	
All dinners	350 to 500

GRAIN PRODUCTS, 1 cup

Macaroni, cooked	155
Macaroni and cheese, canned	230
Macaroni and cheese, homemade	430
Macaroni and cheese, packaged	366
Noodles, egg, cooked	200
Noodle dinner, packaged	181
Pancake, griddle cake, 1 medium	60
Pizza, plain with cheese, 1 slice	185
Rice, enriched, instant ready to serve	180
Rice, enriched, regular, cooked	225
Rice, brown, cooked	272
Rice, Spanish, canned	130
Spaghetti, cooked	155
Spaghetti, tomato sauce/ cheese, canned	260
Spaghetti with meat balls and tomato sauce, canned	260
Spaghetti with meat balls and tomato sauce, homemade	330
Waffle, 1 regular	210

89

	Approx. Calories		Approx. Calories
SALADS		Beans, snap, green,	
Coleslaw, large scoop	165	wax or yellow	15
Chicken salad	202	Beets	28
Chopped egg	205	Broccoli	20
Fruit cocktail, cottage		Brussels sprouts	28
cheese and fruit-		Cabbage	15
flavored gelatin,		Carrots	23
lettuce, salad plate	295	Cauliflower	13
Lettuce and tomato,		Collards	28
no dressing	50	Corn, one ear	70
Potato, large scoop	109	Corn, whole kernel,	
Tossed green,		canned	85
no dressing	20	Cress, 5 to 8 sprigs	3
Tuna, large scoop	180	Kale	15
		Mushrooms, canned	20
SALAD DRESSINGS, 1 Tbs		Onions	30
		Parsnips	50
Bleu cheese	75	Peas, green	58
French	65	Pepper, sweet green, 1	15
Mayonnaise	100	Potato, baked,	
Thousand island	80	1 medium	90
		Potato, boiled,	
VEGETABLES		1 small	40
Fresh, uncooked:		Potatoes, French fried,	
Cabbage, ½ cup	10	fresh, 10	155
Carrots, ½ cup	23	Potatoes, hash	
Celery, 2 stalks	10	browned	229
Cucumber, small pared	15	Potatoes, mashed	
Lettuce, 2 leaves	10	with milk	63
Onions, young green, 6	20	Sauerkraut, canned	23
Onion, mature, 1	40	Spinach	20
Pepper, sweet green, 1	15	Squash, summer	15
Radishes, 4 small	5	Squash, winter,	
Tomato, 1 medium	40	baked and mashed	65
		Sweet potato, baked,	
Cooked or canned, ½ cup:		1 medium	155
Asparagus	15	Sweet potato, canned	118
Beans, green lima	95	Tomato	25
Beans, kidney	102	Turnip	18

	Approx. Calories
DESSERTS AND SWEETS	
Cakes:	
Angel food, ½ of 10-inch-diam. cake	135
Devil's food with chocolate icing, 1/16 of 9-inch layer cake	235
Fruit cake, 1/30 of 8-inch loaf	55
Plain, 1/9 of 9-inch-square cake	315
Pound, ½-inch-thick slice	140
Pastries, 1 piece:	
Brownie with nuts	95
Cupcake, iced	130
Danish pastry	275
Doughnut, plain	125
Eclair, custard filling, chocolate icing	316
Shortcake biscuit with strawberries	399
Cookies, 1:	
Chocolate chip	50
Chocolate fudge sandwich	50
Chocolate graham	58
Chocolate snap	18
Coconut bar	109
Creme sandwich, vanilla and chocolate	50
Fig newton	50

	Approx. Calories
Graham cracker	27
Macaroon	107
Oatmeal with raisins	63
Sugar wafer	26
Vanilla wafer	17
Pies:	
All pieces, 1/7 of 9-inch-diam. pie	300 to 450
Other desserts, ½ cup:	
Apple brown betty	151
Bread pudding with raisins	314
Butterscotch pudding	207
Chocolate pudding	192
Gelatin, fruit-flavored, plain	67
Gelatin with fruit	76
Rice pudding with raisins	141
Tapioca, chocolate	181
Vanilla pudding, minute	133
Other sweets, 1 Tbs:	
Apple butter	26
Butterscotch sauce	102
Chocolate syrup	45
Corn syrup	60
Honey	65
Jams, jellies, marmalade, preserves	50
Maple syrup	50
Molasses, light	50
Sugar, white, granulated	40

91

	Approx. Calories
Candies:	
All candy bars, 1½ to	
2½ ounces	140 to 336
Chocolate cream	51
Chocolate mint, medium	87
Chocolate, bittersweet, 1 ounce	135
Chocolate, sweet, 1 ounce	150
Fudge, 1 ounce	115
Hard candy, 2 squares	38
Marshmallow	25
Peanut brittle, 1 ounce	119
FRUIT	
Apple, fresh	70
Apple, baked	188
Apple sauce, sweetened, ½ cup	155
Apple sauce, unsweetened, ½ cup	50
Apricots, fresh 3 or ¼ lb.	55
Apricots, canned, heavy syrup, 1 cup	220
Apricots, cooked, unsweetened, 1 cup	240
Apricots, dried, uncooked, ½	10
Avocado, fresh, ½ peeled	190
Banana, fresh	100
Blueberries, ½ cup	43
Raspberries, red, ½ cup	35

	Approx. Calories
Strawberries, ½ cup	28
Cantaloupe, fresh, ½ melon	60
Cherries, sweet, fresh, ½ cup	58
Cherries, sweet, canned in light syrup, ½ cup	65
Cherries, maraschino, 1	10
Currants, ½ cup	32
Fig, 1 dried	60
Figs, canned in heavy syrup, 3 small	84
Fruit cocktail, canned in heavy syrup, ½ cup	98
Grapefruit, fresh, ½	45
Grapefruit, canned in heavy syrup, ½ cup	90
Grapes, fresh, ½ cup	48
Honeydew melon, fresh, 3½-ounce slice	33
Lemon, fresh	20
Lime, fresh	28
Orange, fresh	65
Peach, fresh	35
Peaches, canned in heavy syrup, ½ cup	100
Pear, fresh	100
Pears canned in heavy syrup, ½ cup	98
Pineapple, fresh, ½ cup diced	38
Pineapple, canned in heavy syrup, ½ cup	98
Plum, fresh	25
Plums, canned in heavy syrup, ½ cup	103

	Approx. Calories		Approx. Calories
Prunes, cooked, sweetened, ½ cup	172	**NUTS** Almonds, 12	90
Prunes, cooked, unsweetened, ½ cup	148	Brazil, 4	97
		Cashew, 6	84
		Chestnuts, 6 small	58
Prunes, 4 "softenized" dried	70	Coconut, shredded, 1 cup	450
Raisins, dried, ½ cup	240	Mixed nuts, 8	94
Raisins, ½-ounce pkg.	40	Peanut Butter, 1 Tbs	82
Rhubarb, cooked, sweetened, ½ cup	193	Peanuts, roasted, 1 ounce	105
Tangerine, fresh	40	Pecans, 6	104
Watermelon, fresh, 1/16 of 2 lb. melon	115	Pistachio, 30	88
		Walnuts, 10	98

93

FROZEN YOGURT;
or, Where have you been all my life?

February 14, 1975, was the kind of day in New York City when sensible people were staying at home to huddle around fireplaces or, at the very least, radiators.

It was snowing, maybe not hard enough to give pause to Minnesotans, but hard enough to have New Yorkers nervously chattering "blizzard."

Despite the weather, hordes of New Yorkers didn't stay home. They didn't even stay inside. Instead, they were lined up on East 86th Street, waiting to get a taste of a scrumptious new dairy wonder. They were waiting in line for the Dannon company to open its very first Danny-Yo soft-frozen-yogurt shop.

Frozen yogurt in a blizzard! That's what a sensation the new dairy product has been from its beginning right up until now.

It takes most new food items two years or more to catch on. Frozen soft-serve yogurt was an unqualified hit in six months.

"Not since the discovery of chocolate custard ice cream," wrote *Advertising Age* magazine in 1976, "has the soft-serve industry received such a boost as with the debut of soft-frozen yogurt."

The sale of soft-ice-cream machines rose 35 percent in one year—300 to 400 percent at one company. The ultrachic were slurping it up on Manhattan's East Side, and the body-conscious were spooning it down on Malibu Beach. In 1978 approximately forty million pounds of frozen yogurt were consumed.

In July 1976, alone, New York City issued eighteen hundred new licenses to soft-yogurt operators. Existing shops accused newcomers of starting spy wars on their operations.

"We see them coming in all the time," one Wall Street frozen yogurteer complained. "They pretend to be customers, but really they just want to steal our ideas and set up their own frozen-yogurt business."

Ideas like frozen yogurt in chocolate cups doused with crème de menthe; frozen yogurt in whole-wheat cones sprinkled with almonds and coconut; frozen yogurt cuddled up in avocado halves; frozen yogurt in crepes, topped with fresh fruit; frozen yogurt shaken up with cranberry or papaya juice.

Here was surely a product whose time had come. It was ice cream without guilt. It was yummy. It was delicious. And people wanted more.

Food historians claim that Marco Polo was treated to frozen yogurt in the mountains of Far East. If he was, it didn't catch on. In 1968, however, Dannon developed its Danny Freeze, soft frozen yogurt that it tested in several stores and restaurants. The reception was great but stopped there—Dannon found itself too busy expanding its regular yogurt business to market a new product. So Danny Freeze was "put on the back burner," as Juan Metzger put it, although put in the back freezer was more like it.

In 1972, a small eating place, the Spa, on Harvard Square in Cambridge, Massachusetts, asked a dairy company in the area to come up with "something different" for its customers. The company did, and soon the Spa found itself coping with long lines of hungry students eager to wait for that "something different," frozen yogurt, at all hours of the day and night.

Bloomingdale's, the very trendy New York department store, picked up very quickly on the frozen-yogurt phenomenon, and started serving it at its Forty Carrots restaurant. Before long, Dannon decided it was time to bring Danny Freeze, renamed Danny-Yo, out of the freezer and into the ice-cream cone.

Today you can get soft frozen yogurt at hundreds of stores across the country and hard frozen yogurt in your supermarket ice-cream case.

The dairy industry is still not sure if frozen yogurt is a novelty or if it is here to stay—there is no history on the product, and sales have slipped a bit from the initial burst. Those of us out there eating frozen yogurt, on the other hand, know it's a way of life. What a great way to get a delicious dessert with fewer calories than ice cream and far less fat.

"That's why I like it," one devotee explained between licks. "It's less fattening. It's also got a tang that you don't find in regular ice cream."

(I do have a friend who unabashedly defies eating custom by having frozen yogurt for breakfast.)

Another plus to frozen yogurt—at least the kind made by the Dannon method of pasteurization before inoculation—is that it has the healthful attributes of regular yogurt. The bacteria aren't killed by freezing; they kind of hibernate, waking up when the yogurt melts in your body.

Those who want not only taste, but also a minimum of additives, should be cautious about buying just any frozen yogurt. A lot of manufacturers throw in all manner of additives—sodium citrate, locust-bean gum, sodium carboxymethycellulose, mono- and di-glycerides, polysorbate 80, and for coloring, beets, annatto, and tumeric extract.

Dannon adds only a tiny bit of gelatin so that the yogurt won't crystallize when frozen. Why mess up a good thing with a lot of goop?

If you have one of the new super-duper ice-cream makers, such as the Waring Ice Cream Parlor, you can make your own yogurt desserts. If you don't, some delicious frozen concoctions appear in the dessert-recipe

99

section of this book, along with recipes using ice-cream machines.

Whether you make it yourself or buy it in the store, there's no getting around it—frozen yogurt is a delightful way to finish any meal.

RECIPES

INTRODUCTION

Enjoying a food in its plain or purest form can be an immense pleasure—crunching into that just-picked autumn-red apple is a delight! A hard-boiled egg, its center still warm, tastes terrific. But an egg, after all, is an egg, until it is an omelette smothered with asparagus and white sauce, or until it is sandwiched between an English muffin and Canadian bacon and lathered with hollandaise, or until it is beaten to perfection and allowed to ascend to the heights of a souffl'e.

And so it is with yogurt. From the container it is a pleasure, a delight, but so much more can be done with it. Adventuring adds to enjoyment.

Americans are late-blooming discoverers of the treat of cooking with yogurt. The Turks, Greeks, Russians, and Armenians think nothing of spicing, stirring, blending, and baking with it. That's a part of their cultural culinary repertoire. We have just begun to catch on to yogurt dolloping and dashing.

As Anthelme Brillat-Savarin once said, "The discovery of a new dish does more for human happiness than the discovery of a new star."

What follows are some happy discoveries for you—yogurt in appetizers, soups, salads, entr'ees, vegetables, and, best of all, desserts.

Good eating to you, your family, and your lucky guests.

APPETIZERS

YOGURT SEAFOOD DIP

Shrimp and lobster don't have to be served with a tomato-y sauce, as this dip so clearly and deliciously proves.

1 cup yogurt, well stirred
1⅓ cups cucumber, peeled and chopped
2 tsp salt
1 tsp sugar
1 tsp aromatic bitters

Combine all ingredients. Chill. Serve with shrimp or medallions of rock lobster.

2 cups

ZIPPY SAUCE

This makes a wonderful party-appetizer dish instead of chips, nuts, and the usual calorie-laden munchies. And if you must chomp while watching TV, vegetables in Zippy Sauce are both healthful and delicious.

1 cup plain yogurt, well stirred
¼ cup tomato catsup
1 Tbs finely chopped scallions
1 tsp onion juice
½ tsp Worcestershire sauce
¼ tsp Tabasco sauce
salt to taste

Mix all ingredients. Chill. Serve with raw vegetables.

1¼ cups

RUSSIAN FONDUE

Don't wait until you're huddling around a châlet fire after a cold day of skiing to dip into this dish. It's a tangy, zippy fondue to be eaten the year round.

1 clove garlic, crushed
½ cup white wine
1 pound finely grated, aged Swiss or Cheddar cheese
⅛ tsp freshly ground pepper
1 cup plain yogurt, well stirred
French bread, cut in bite-size cubes

Rub fondue pot with garlic. Place pot over alcohol burner. When hot, add wine. Gradually add cheese, stirring constantly until melted and smooth. Stir in yogurt and pepper. Keep flame low—fondue should not boil. Spear bread cubes and dip them into fondue. If fondue thickens, thin with a little heated wine.

HERRING IN DILL YOGURT SAUCE

Why be a slave to store-bought, bottled herring? Making your own variation is a cinch—and the result is memorable. The tastes of yogurt and herring are superbly complementary.

  1 cup plain yogurt, well stirred
 ½ cup vinegar
 ⅓ cup oil
 ¼ cup dry white wine
 ½ tsp sugar
  4 fillets pickled herring, cut in 1-inch slices
  2 medium onions, thinly sliced
  1 clove garlic, minced
12 peppercorns
  4 bay leaves
    sprigs of fresh dill

Combine yogurt and next four ingredients. In two widemouth jars, arrange alternating layers of herring and onion slices. Distribute garlic, peppercorns, bay leaves, and dill among the layers. Pour in yogurt mixture. With fork, tilt herring so yogurt mixture covers all ingredients. Cover jars. Refrigerate several days before serving.

AVOCADO DIP

Avocados never had it so good—and, as Marcia Anderson says, neither have your taste buds.

2 large ripe avocados, mashed
2 cups plain yogurt, well stirred
2 Tbs chopped chives
1 tsp salt
¼ tsp oregano
½ tsp dill weed

Combine all ingredients; mix thoroughly. Cover and chill. Serve with cucumber and celery sticks.

CLAM DIP

Has clam dip become a ho-hum party snack de rigeur? It doesn't have to be, and it isn't when made with yogurt and cream cheese. If you want an even spicier dip, add a few extra drops of Tabasco.

1 cup plain yogurt, well stirred
1 3-ounce package cream cheese, softened
1 Tbs lemon juice
1 6½-ounce can chopped clams, drained
1 Tbs minced onion
½ tsp chopped, fresh basil (or ¼ tsp dried)
½ tsp chopped, fresh tarragon (or ¼ tsp dried)
¼ tsp Worcestershire sauce
¼ tsp minced garlic
   few drops Tabasco sauce

Combine yogurt, cream cheese, and lemon juice; mix thoroughly. Stir in remaining ingredients. Chill. Serve with raw vegetables or crackers.

About 2 cups

SOUPS

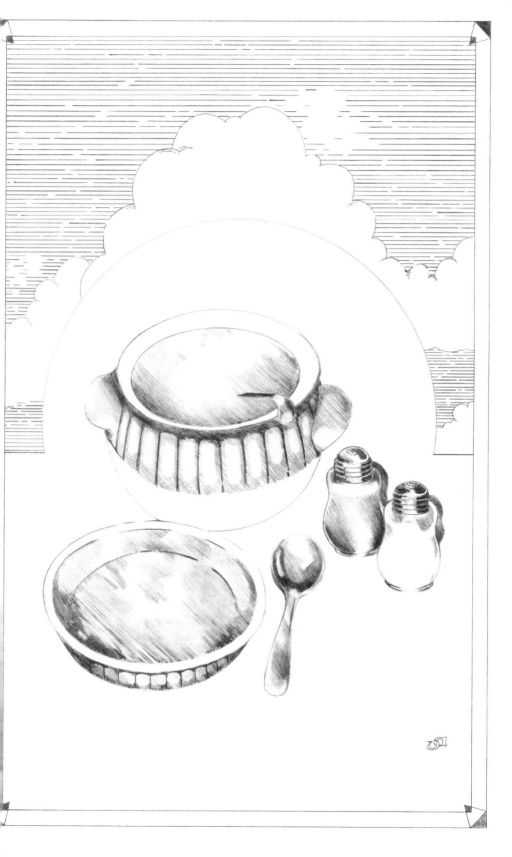

CURRIED SUMMER SOUP

All the different tastes and textures of this soup make it both interesting and delicious. Guests will request it again and again.

3 cups yogurt, well stirred
½ cup milk or light cream
1 egg, hard cooked, chopped
1 cup cucumber, chopped
½ cup scallions, chopped
½ cup raisins
1 tsp salt
¼ tsp pepper
1 tsp curry
  water
1 Tbs parsley, chopped
1 Tbs dill, fresh, chopped

In a bowl, combine the yogurt, cream, egg, cucumber, scallions, raisins, salt, and pepper. Dissolve the curry in a small amount of water and stir into the yogurt mixture. Refrigerate for 3 to 4 hours.

Serve with the parsley and dill sprinkled over it as garnish.

6 to 8 servings

TURKISH SOUP

A simple but good soup that again proves that the Turks know what they are about when it comes to cooking with yogurt.

1 cup onion, chopped
2 Tbs butter or margarine
4 cups chicken broth
3 Tbs raw rice
¼ cup mint, chopped
2 cups plain yogurt, well stirred
   salt and pepper

In medium saucepan, sauté onion in butter until tender. Add chicken broth and rice. Cover and simmer 10 minutes. Add mint; simmer 5 minutes more. Stir in yogurt; heat to serving temperature over low heat. Do not boil. Salt and pepper to taste.

4 servings

WATERCRESS SOUP

There's nothing more refreshing than cold watercress soup on a hot day. Combine the sharpness of the vegetable with the smoothness of the yogurt, and voila! the mixture is something to savor.

1 to 1½ cups chicken broth
    ¾ cup chopped onion
    ½ cup minced watercress leaves
    1 cup plain yogurt, well stirred
       salt and pepper
    4 tsp grated lemon rind

Combine broth and onion in saucepan; cover and simmer 10 minutes. Pour into electric blender; blend until smooth. Return to saucepan. Add watercress; simmer 5 minutes. Chill. Before serving, stir in yogurt. Add salt and pepper to taste. Garnish with grated lemon rind.

2 to 4 servings

TOMATO CHILI SOUP

Another hot-day favorite. If you're the type who enjoys having your tongue spiced-out, increase the amount of hot chili peppers. And don't fret that it will increase hot-day discomfort. Spicy foods will make you sweat and actually cool you down.

         4 ripe tomatoes
         1 onion, finely chopped
        ¼ cup parsley, chopped
1 to 1½ Tbs hot chili peppers, diced
         3 cups plain yogurt, well stirred
            salt
         4 radishes, thinly sliced
        ½ cup cucumber, peeled and chopped

Peel, seed, and coarsely chop tomatoes. Combine tomatoes, onion, parsley, and chili peppers; refrigerate at least 2 hours. Stir in yogurt. Salt to taste. Garnish with radish slices and chopped cucumber.

4 servings

SPINACH SOUP

You don't have to be Popeye to go crazy over this use of spinach.

1 cup chopped onion
2 large cloves garlic, minced
2 Tbs butter or margarine
4 cups chicken broth
2 tsp cornstarch
2 Tbs cold water
1 10-ounce package frozen spinach
2 cups plain yogurt, well stirred
salt

In medium saucepan, sauté onion and garlic in butter until soft. Add chicken broth. Bring to boil. Dissolve cornstarch in cold water. Stir into broth. Cook, stirring, 5 minutes. Add spinach. Return to boil. Reduce heat. Simmer, uncovered, 5 minutes. (If cooked longer spinach will lose the green color.) Remove from heat. Stir in yogurt, first mixed with some of the broth. Pour about 2 cups of soup into blender container at a time. Cover. Blend until smooth. Pour blended soup into a second saucepan. Repeat until all is blended. Reheat over low heat. Do not boil.

6 to 8 servings

SALADS

MAST VA KHIAR
(Persian Yogurt and Cucumber Salad)

If you're looking for an extra-refreshing summer salad, this is your ticket. It's cool and piquant—delightful on hot, muggy days.

1 cup plain yogurt, well stirred
1 large cucumber, peeled, seeded, and chopped
1 Tbs fresh dill (or ½ tsp dill weed)
  salt and pepper to taste
  Boston lettuce leaves
1 cucumber, thinly sliced

In a small bowl, combine yogurt, chopped cucumber, and dill. Season to taste with salt and pepper. Chill thoroughly. Just before serving, place lettuce and sliced cucumber on salad plates; spoon on yogurt mixture.

1 serving as a luncheon entrée
2 to 3 servings as an appetizer

ORANGE AND GRAPE SALAD

Some salads are sweet enough to be served as dessert. This is one of those.

3 Tbs orange juice
2 Tbs honey
1 Tbs lemon juice
1 Tbs mint, fresh, or a pinch of dried mint
1 cup yogurt
2 seedless oranges, peeled and sectioned
½ lb. seedless grapes

Mix the orange juice, honey, lemon juice, and mint. Stir in the yogurt. Fold in the oranges and grapes. Chill.

4 servings

SPINACH SALAD

Thursday's Restaurant former chef Stanley Kramer has his way with spinach salad, and the result is memorable.

5 ounces fresh spinach, washed and
trimmed
2 to 4 fresh mushrooms, sliced
1 scallion, sliced
4 slices bacon, cooked, drained, and
crumbled
½ hard-cooked egg, chopped
1 cup plain yogurt, well stirred
1½ tsp lemon juice
½ tsp fresh chopped mint

Combine spinach, mushrooms, scallion, bacon, and egg. Stir together yogurt, lemon juice, and mint; pour over bacon mixture. Toss gently.

1 serving as a luncheon entrée
2 to 3 servings as an appetizer

YOGURT SALAD GEMS

Yogurt and gelatin work magic in a salad, and it's very colorful.

1 6-ounce package lime-flavored gelatin
1 cup boiling water
1¼ cups cold water
2 cups vanilla yogurt, well stirred
  lettuce leaves
1½ cups cantaloupe balls

Dissolve the gelatin in the boiling water. Pour ⅔ cup of this into an 8-inch-square pan and stir in the cold water. Mix the yogurt with the remaining gelatin and pour into a second 8-inch pan.

Chill both pans until firm, about 4 hours.

Cut into cubes and arrange on lettuce-lined salad plates with the melon balls.

8 servings

CUCUMBER BORANI

Thanks, thanks, and more thanks to Stanley Kramer, former head chef at Thursday's Restaurant in New York City, for his version of this classic dish.

1 large cucumber, peeled, seeded, and sliced
  salt
1 cup plain yogurt, well stirred
½ cup sliced onions
1 clove garlic, crushed
1½ tsp lemon juice
½ tsp fresh chopped mint
  lettuce leaves
  walnuts

Sprinkle cucumbers with salt. Let stand 10 to 15 minutes; drain well. Add yogurt, onions, garlic, lemon juice, and mint. Toss well. Arrange on lettuce leaves. Garnish with walnuts.

2 servings

JOYCE PANITZ'S PICK-ME-UP

Joyce is one of those perky, energetic, healthy-looking people, and her pick-me-up is part of the secret.

1 cup yogurt
⅓ cup low-fat cottage cheese
  soy nuts, unsalted
1 Tbs honey
  fresh fruit

Combine the ingredients in a small bowl.

1 serving

SALAD DRESSINGS

Yogurt couldn't be more perfect for salad dressings. Its tart richness is a fantastic base for cheeses, nuts, herbs, fruits, and spices. What follows are some favorites, but don't be shy. Experiment and enjoy!

LIVELY SALAD DRESSING

A creation of Stanley Kramer, former chef of Thursday's.

1 cup plain yogurt, well stirred
1 cup mayonnaise
1½ cups salad oil
½ cup onions, minced
2 Tbs lemon juice
1½ Tbs chopped chives
1 Tbs fresh minced parsley
1 tsp Dijon mustard
1 hard-cooked egg, chopped
1 clove garlic, crushed
salt and pepper

In medium bowl, combine yogurt and mayonnaise. Slowly mix in salad oil, beating constantly. Stir in onions, lemon juice, chives, parsley, mustard, egg, and garlic. Add salt and pepper to taste. Serve on greens of your choice or on potato salad.

about 4½ cups

BLUE BLEU CHEESE DRESSING
(aka Bleu Blue Cheese Dressing)

⅓ cup mayonnaise
⅓ cup bleu cheese, crumbled
2 Tbs milk
⅛ tsp thyme, ground
1 small clove garlic, minced
   a dash of white pepper
1 cup yogurt

Stir together the mayonnaise, bleu cheese, milk, thyme, garlic, and white pepper. Fold in the yogurt. Chill.

about 1½ cups

PECAN DRESSING

⅓ cup mayonnaise
⅓ cup chopped pecans
¼ cup light corn syrup
1 cup plain yogurt, well stirred

Stir together the mayonnaise, pecans, and corn syrup. Fold in the yogurt. Chill. Serve over fresh fruit.

1½ cups

SPECIAL THOUSAND ISLAND DRESSING

⅓ cup mayonnaise
½ cup chili sauce
1 egg, hard cooked, finely chopped
1 Tbs stuffed, chopped olives
1 Tbs dill pickle, chopped
1 tsp onion, grated
1 cup plain yogurt, well stirred

Stir together the mayonnaise, egg, chili sauce, olive, pickle, and onion. Fold in the yogurt. Chill.

2 cups

CUCUMBER PARSLEY DRESSING

½ cup mayonnaise
1 cup cucumber, peeled, seeded, chopped
2 Tbs fresh parsley, minced
1 small clove garlic, minced
¼ tsp salt
⅛ tsp pepper
1 cup plain yogurt, well stirred

Stir together the mayonnaise, cucumber, parsley, garlic, salt, and pepper. Fold in the yogurt and chill.

2⅔ cups

ENTRÉES

BEEF GOULASH

A Hungarian favorite with a saucy twist. Yogurt is used instead of sour cream to give the dish a slightly different but still delicious character.

3 Tbs butter or margarine
4 cups onions, thinly sliced
2 lbs. boneless beef, cut in 1-inch cubes
2 Tbs Hungarian paprika
1 tsp salt
¼ cup beef bouillon
2 tsp cornstarch
2 Tbs water
2 cups plain yogurt, well stirred

Melt the butter in a Dutch oven over medium heat. Sauté the onions until they are golden brown. Add the beef, the paprika, the salt, and the bouillon to the onions and bring to a boil. Cover and simmer for 3 to 4 hours or until the meat is very tender.

Combine the cornstarch with the water; add to meat mixture. Cook, stirring constantly, until mixture thickens and boils. Stir in yogurt.

6 servings

133

LEMONY-GINGER CHICKEN

Something this good shouldn't be this easy. It is. It is so full flavored and so lemony that it should carry a warning: THIS MAY BE HABIT FORMING.
The varying tastes—sweet, sour, spicy—playing off each other make this a delight!

4 chicken cutlets
½ cup butter or margarine
2 Tbs lemon juice
¾ tsp paprika
¼ tsp salt
1 cup plain yogurt, well stirred
1 tsp powdered ginger
1 tsp grated lemon peel
1 large garlic clove, crushed
¼ cup Parmesan cheese, grated
    lemon, sliced, for garnish

In large skillet, brown chicken breasts in butter. Sprinkle with lemon juice, paprika, and salt. Cover and simmer about 15 minutes or until tender. Transfer chicken to warm baking dish. Combine yogurt, ginger, lemon peel, and garlic. Spread over chicken. Sprinkle with cheese. Bake in 375-degree oven about 10 minutes or until heated through. Garnish with lemon slices.

4 servings

STEAK WITH YOGURT SAUCE

The robustness of steak is well complemented by this spicy sauce. Serve with rice or noodles and an unadorned green vegetable.

   4 Tbs peanut oil
   2 lbs. steak, boneless (preferably a strip steak or some other high-quality cut), ¼ inch thick
   1 cup onions, minced
1½ Tbs flour
   2 tsp coriander, ground
   1 tsp ginger, ground
   ¼ tsp cardamon, ground
   ¼ tsp cumin, ground
   ¼ tsp salt
   ⅔ cup beef bouillon
   2 cups plain yogurt, well stirred

Put 3 tablespoons of the oil in a skillet and brown the steak over moderate heat. Remove the steak to a platter and keep it warm. To the skillet add the remaining 1 tablespoon of oil and the onions. Lower the heat and cook, covered, for approximately 10 minutes, or until the onions are soft.

Add the flour, coriander, ginger, cardamon, cumin, and salt. Cook, stirring, for 1 minute. Stir in the bouillon and bring to a boil. Lower the heat and gradually add the yogurt, stirring constantly. Simmer, stirring, for 10 minutes or until the sauce is thick.

Add the steak and cook gently for a minute or two until heated thoroughly.

4 servings

YOGURTY LAMB STEW

Stews such as this are eaten in almost every Middle Eastern country, for good reason. The yogurt added to the sauce gives the stew a rich, distinctive flavor.

2 Tbs olive oil
2½ lbs. boneless lamb shoulder, cubed
1 cup onions, chopped
3 cloves garlic, minced
1 cup chicken broth
1½ tsp coriander, ground
½ tsp salt
¼ tsp pepper
2 Tbs cornstarch
¼ cup milk
1 egg, lightly beaten
2 cups plain yogurt, well stirred

Heat the oil in a large Dutch oven and sauté the meat until it is brown. Add the onions and garlic and continue to cook until onions are tender. Stir in the chicken broth, coriander, salt, and pepper. Simmer, covered, 1½ hours or until the meat is tender.

Combine the cornstarch and milk, mixing to a smooth paste. Stir into the stew. Cook, stirring constantly, until the sauce thickens.

Beat together the egg and the yogurt. Stir in 1 tablespoon of the hot lamb sauce. Stir the yogurt into the Dutch oven a few tablespoons at a time. Keep the stew warm.

6 servings

POACHED EGGS WITH TARRAGON AND YOGURT

Robert Lynd once said, "There are nine ways of poaching eggs, and each of them is worse than the other." Poor man! He obviously never tried this version of poached eggs.

6 eggs, poached
2 cups plain yogurt, well stirred
1 tsp paprika
2 tsp chopped fresh tarragon (or ½ teaspoon dried)
salt
parsley sprigs

Arrange the eggs on a hot serving dish. In a saucepan, mix the yogurt, paprika, and tarragon. Salt to taste. Stir over low heat until warm. Spoon the mixture over the eggs. Garnish with parsley.

6 servings

FISH BAKE

An especially tasty and foolproof way to prepare fish. Even if you've botched every previous attempt at serving denizens of the deep, this recipe will turn out well.

3   cups hot seasoned mashed potatoes
1   egg, well beaten
2   cups plain yogurt, well stirred
2   cups flaked, cold cooked fish
1   green chili, minced
1   onion, minced
1   Tbs chopped fresh parsley
½   tsp salt
1   tsp chopped fresh dill (or ¼ teaspoon dried)
¼   cup chopped chives

Mix together the potatoes and the egg. Spread half of mixture in a greased casserole. Mix the yogurt with the remaining ingredients, except the chives. Spoon mixture evenly over the potatoes. Top with remaining potatoes. Bake in 350-degree oven 20 to 30 minutes or until browned. Sprinkle with chives before serving.

4 servings

SMORGASBORD MEATBALLS

*Meat balls—along with Ingrid Bergman and the Volvo—
rank high in Sweden's contributions to Western civilization.
This version, in its rich yogurt sauce, will serve four for
dinner or make a great addition to a buffet table.*

1½ pounds ground meat (combination of beef,
      pork, and veal)
½ cup soft bread crumbs
½ cup milk
¼ cup minced onion
2 Tbs chopped fresh parsley
1½ tsp salt
1 tsp Worcestershire sauce
⅛ tsp freshly ground pepper
1 egg, slightly beaten
¼ cup butter or margarine
1 cup plain yogurt, well stirred

Mix together all the ingredients except butter and
yogurt. Shape into balls the size of a walnut. Heat butter
in a large skillet; brown the meatballs on all sides. Just
before serving stir in the yogurt. Heat but do not boil.

4 servings

VEAL PAPRIKA

Despite what your mother may have told you, veal paprika doesn't have to be made with sour cream. Yogurt gives it an extra zing and verve you're sure to like.

1 veal cutlet, about 1½ pounds, or 4 thick loin veal chops
½ tsp salt
⅛ tsp freshly ground pepper
2 eggs
1 Tbs milk
⅔ cup fine bread crumbs
1 Tbs oil
1 Tbs butter or margarine
2 cups plain yogurt, well stirred
2 Tbs paprika
½ Tbs garlic, minced

Sprinkle the veal with the salt and pepper. Beat the eggs with the milk. Brush the veal generously with the egg mixture and dip in the bread crumbs. Heat the oil and butter in large oval casserole. Brown the veal on each side. Mix the yogurt, paprika, and garlic together and pour over the veal. Bake, covered, in preheated 325-degree oven about 1¼ hours or until veal is tender.

4 servings

CHICKEN MALAYSIA

*Columbus sailed the ocean blue in search of spices for a dish
like this. What second-rate consolation it must have been,
merely to discover America.*

1½ tsp chili powder
1 Tbs ground coriander
½ tsp ground cumin
1 tsp sugar
¾ tsp salt
¼ tsp freshly ground pepper
1 large clove garlic, minced
3 Tbs oil
2 cups plain yogurt, well stirred
2 broiling chickens, 2½ pounds each, cut into
   serving pieces

In a small skillet cook the spices, sugar, salt, pepper,
and garlic in oil about 1 minute, stirring constantly.
Add this mixture to the yogurt. Blend well. Cover
chicken with the mixture. Marinate 1 hour or more,
turning often. Arrange the chicken in a greased shallow
baking pan and spoon the marinade over it. Bake in
preheated 350-degree oven about 35 to 45 minutes.

6 servings

TACOS CON YOGURT

Tangy and tempting! As Paul Busby says, "These tacos would get Montezuma's mind off revenge!"

12 corn tortillas
hot oil
1 lb. grated Monterey Jack cheese
1 4-ounce can peeled whole green chilis
salt
pepper
1½ cups tomato sauce
½ cup white sauce
3 cups plain yogurt, well stirred

Dip tortillas in hot oil. On each place about ¼ cup cheese, ⅓ chili, salt, pepper, and 2 tablespoons tomato sauce. Roll. Place, seam side down, in a large baking dish. Mix white sauce and yogurt. Spoon over all. Bake in preheated 350-degree oven for 30 minutes.

6 servings

VEGETABLES

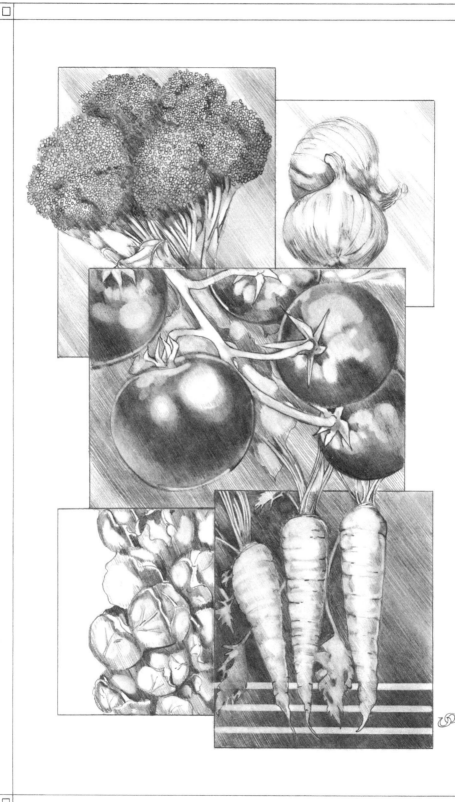

STUFFED POTATOES

Take some of the sin—and calories—out of stuffed baked potatoes, without losing any of their richness.

4 baking potatoes
5 Tbs butter
1 cup plain yogurt, well stirred
   a pinch of dill weed, crushed
½ tsp salt

Preheat oven to 400 degrees.

Clean the potatoes and bake for one hour. (Prick the potatoes after 20 minutes.) Halve the potatoes lengthwise and remove the insides without breaking the skins.

Mash the pulp and add the butter, yogurt, dill, and salt, whipping until most of the lumps are gone. Spoon the pulp mixture into the skins. Lower the oven temperature to 350 degrees and bake the potatoes for 10 minutes.

4 servings

LINDA'S VEGIE PIE

When Linda invites you to her house for dinner, you involuntarily start salivating. She is a superb and natural cook. When her son became a vegetarian, Linda became even more interested in vegetables and more adept with them.

Serve this as a side dish or as a main course. Either way it's equally satisfying.

4 Tbs butter or margarine
1 cup scallions, finely chopped
1 cup broccoli, finely chopped
½ cup onion, finely chopped
1 cup carrots, finely chopped
1 cup leeks, finely chopped
2 Tbs flour
2 Tbs white wine
1 9-inch pie shell (recipe below)
2 eggs, beaten
1 cup plain yogurt, well stirred

In a deep skillet, melt the butter and sauté the scallions, broccoli, onion, and carrots for 3 to 4 minutes over a medium heat.

Add the leeks, flour, and wine, tossing until thoroughly mixed. Put this mixture into the pie crust and spread the beaten eggs over it. The yogurt is spread on top of the eggs.

Bake for 50 minutes and serve hot.

4 servings as an entrée
6 to 8 servings as a side dish

PIE SHELL

1 cup flour, sifted
½ tsp salt
4 Tbs butter
2 Tbs shortening
4 to 6 Tbs water, cold

Sift flour and salt into a large bowl. With either a pastry blender or two knives, cut the butter and shortening into the flour until it forms pea-sized lumps. One tablespoon at a time, add the cold water, mixing lightly with a fork, until the flour is moistened and forms a ball.

Lightly flour the ball and a rolling pin. Place the ball in the center of a floured surface (waxed paper will do). Starting from the center of the ball, roll the dough to the edges until it is a 12-inch circle. (If the dough isn't perfectly circular, don't worry.) Put the rolling pin in the center of the dough and lift half the dough over it.

Transfer the dough, draped over the pin, to a 9-inch pie plate. (If your dough wasn't perfectly circular, you may have some bare spots on your pie plate. In that case, cut off some of the overlap from another place and knead it into the bare spot.)

STANLEY KRAMER'S RICE PILAF

That marvelous former head chef of Thursday's in New York does it again with this perfect way to take the blahs out of rice.

2 Tbs butter
⅔ cup onions, minced
2 cups long-grain rice
1 bay leaf
3 cups chicken broth
½ tsp salt
⅛ tsp pepper
2 cups plain yogurt, well stirred
1½ cups Cheddar cheese, shredded
a dash of Tabasco sauce
buttered bread crumbs (recipe opposite)

Preheat oven to 375 degrees.

In a large ovenproof saucepan, melt the butter. Add the onions and sauté until tender, about 3 to 5 minutes. Stir in the rice and bay leaf, cooking until the rice is well coated. Add the chicken broth, salt, and pepper. Bring to a boil.

Cover the saucepan and bake for 18 to 20 minutes. Remove from oven and stir in 1 cup of the yogurt, 1 cup of the shredded cheese, and the Tabasco sauce. Remove the bay leaf. Mix well.

Spoon the mixture into a 2-quart baking dish. Spread on the remaining yogurt and sprinkle on the remaining cheese. Top with buttered bread crumbs. Bake for another 15 minutes, or until the top is golden-brown.

6 to 8 servings

148

BUTTERED BREAD CRUMBS

1 Tbs butter
1 cup bread crumbs, fresh (about 2 slices)

Melt the butter in a skillet. Add the bread crumbs and stir until well coated.
(Buttered bread crumbs may be refrigerated and re-heated.)

ZINGY STUFFED POTATOES

Want a little more zip in those stuffed spuds? This recipe is absolutely great.

4 baking potatoes
2 Tbs butter
1 cup plain yogurt, well stirred
½ tsp salt
¼ cup bacon, cooked and crumbled
¼ cup sharp Cheddar cheese, grated

Preheat oven to 400 degrees.

Clean the potatoes and bake for about one hour. (Prick them after 20 minutes.) Halve potatoes lengthwise and remove the insides without breaking the skins.

Mash the pulp and add the butter, yogurt, and salt, whipping until most of the lumps are gone. Spoon the pulp mixture into the skins. Sprinkle 1 tablespoon each of bacon and cheese onto each potato half.

Lower the oven temperature to 350 degrees and bake the potatoes for 10 minutes or until the cheese has melted.

4 servings

BRUSSELS SPROUTS À LA JENNIFER

Even those who don't usually include Brussels sprouts on their menus will like this way of serving the vegetable. It's also a great company dish—a snap to prepare, but it looks as if you worked for hours.

> 1 lb. brussels sprouts, trimmed
> 1 cup tomatoes, stewed
> 1 cup plain yogurt, well stirred
> ½ cup Cheddar cheese, grated
> 2 tsp flour
>   salt and pepper

Preheat oven to 350 degrees.

Cook the trimmed brussels sprouts in 1 inch of boiling water for approximately 8 to 10 minutes, until barely tender. Drain. Place them in an oiled or buttered casserole. Cover with the stewed tomatoes.

Combine the yogurt, cheese, and flour and mix well. Add salt and pepper to taste. Smear over the brussels sprouts and tomatoes.

Cover the casserole and bake for 15 minutes.

4 servings

CARAWAY CABBAGE

Cabbage often gets short shrift in American kitchens, the thinking being, "If it's not cole slaw, it's not cabbage." Caraway Cabbage is sure to change your attitude.

2 Tbs vegetable oil
1 small green cabbage, shredded
2 cups chopped raw apple
½ tsp caraway seeds
⅛ tsp ground allspice
1 cup plain yogurt, well stirred
　 salt and pepper

In large skillet heat the oil. Sauté the cabbage until it wilts. Add apple and spices. Cover and simmer until cabbage is tender. Remove from heat. Stir in the yogurt and add salt and pepper to taste.

4 servings

BAKED ONIONS

Tired of steak and fries or roast beef and baked potatoes?
This is an imaginative side-dish alternative.

6 large onions, sliced
3 Tbs butter or margarine
1 cup plain yogurt, well stirred
3 egg yolks, well beaten
1 Tbs chopped parsley
¾ tsp salt
⅛ tsp freshly ground pepper
⅛ tsp thyme
⅛ tsp summer savory
⅛ tsp oregano
½ cup soft bread crumbs
⅓ cup grated Cheddar cheese

In large skillet sauté the onions in the butter until crisp-tender. Place in shallow buttered 1-quart baking dish. Mix the yogurt, egg yolks, and seasonings and pour over onions. Sprinkle with bread crumbs and cheese. Bake in 350-degree oven about 30 to 40 minutes or until egg mixture is set and top is browned.

4 servings

SAUCED SQUASH FRITTERS

These fritters can be served as a side dish with dinner or as an adventurous Sunday brunch.

       1 cup flour
1 to 1½ tsp baking soda
      ½ tsp salt
       1 egg
      ½ cup water
       3 medium summer squash, sliced thin
          oil for deep frying
       2 cups plain yogurt, well stirred (at room
          temperature)
       1 clove garlic, minced

Combine the flour, baking soda, and ½ teaspoon salt. Beat egg with water. Stir into flour mixture until smooth. Dip squash slices in batter. Fry in deep fat heated to 375 degrees until golden. Drain on paper towels; keep warm. Combine yogurt, garlic, and remaining salt to taste. Serve squash with sauce.

6 servings

DESSERTS

Vanilla pod & flower

COFFEE

BOYSENBERRY DELICIOUS

And it couldn't be better.

2 envelopes unflavored gelatin
⅔ cup sugar
3 eggs, separated
1 cup milk
2 cups boysenberry yogurt, well stirred
1 cup heavy cream, whipped

In a medium saucepan, mix the gelatin and ⅓ cup sugar. In a bowl, beat the egg yolks with the milk; blend into the gelatin and sugar. Stir over a low heat until the gelatin dissolves, about five minutes. Whisk in the yogurt.

Chill, stirring occasionally, until the mixture mounds slightly when dropped from a spoon.

In a medium bowl, beat the egg whites until soft peaks form. Gradually add the remaining sugar, beating until stiff. Fold the gelatin mixture into the beaten egg whites. Then fold in the whipped cream. Turn into individual dessert dishes and chill until set.

8 to 10 servings

BULGARIAN YOGURT CAKE

The Bulgarians have a way with—and a penchant for— yogurt cakes. This one is made even more yummy by the addition of a yogurt-vanilla sauce.

2 cups sifted flour
2 tsp baking powder
½ tsp baking soda
½ tsp salt
½ cup butter
⅔ cup sugar
2 eggs
1 cup plain yogurt, well stirred
2 tsp grated lemon rind
   yogurt-vanilla sauce (recipe opposite)

Sift together the flour, baking powder, baking soda, and salt. Reserve. In a large mixing bowl cream the butter and sugar together until light and fluffy. Beat in eggs, one at a time. Stir in the yogurt and lemon rind, then stir in the dry ingredients.

Pour this batter into a greased and floured 9-inch-square cake pan. Bake in a 350-degree oven about 40 to 50 minutes. Test for doneness by inserting a toothpick into the center. If it comes out clean, the cake is done. (Don't worry if the cake seems too moist; the finished dessert does not have the exact texture of ordinary cake.)

Serve warm with the yogurt-vanilla sauce.

YOGURT-VANILLA SAUCE

This should be made shortly before serving.

1 egg, separated
1 cup vanilla yogurt, well stirred
1 Tbs sugar

Beat the egg yolk in a medium-sized bowl until it is
lemony colored. Add the yogurt, mixing well. Beat the
egg white at a slow speed until it is foamy. Add the sugar
and beat at a higher speed until it forms stiff peaks.

Fold this into the yogurt mixture.

MRS. FOSTER'S YOGURT PIE

. . . an outstanding restaurant Holiday magazine
Pearl Byrd Foster . . . has made a veritable
art of American cookery. Town and Country
Four stars. New York Times

These are only a few of the raves that Mr. and Mrs. Foster's Place, at 242 East 81st Street, in New York City, has deservedly received. So you'd expect that a yogurt pie created by Mrs. Foster would be wonderful; however, this one is almost beyond belief.

1 Tbs gelatin, unflavored*
2 egg yolks, slightly beaten
¼ cup water, cold
¼ cup milk
1 tsp vanilla extract
8 ounces Neufchâtel cheese, room temperature†
8 ounces cream cheese, room temperature
1 tsp molasses
1 Tbs clover honey
2 cups yogurt
1 graham-cracker-crumb shell (recipe opposite)

---

*If you like a softer filling, use less gelatin.
†You may substitute an additional 8 ounces of cream cheese if Neufchâtel is not available.

In the top of a double boiler, sprinkle the gelatin onto the water. Place the pot over hot water and dissolve the gelatin. Add the milk to the slightly beaten egg yolks and cook with the gelatin over gently boiling water until it coats a spoon. Set aside to cool.

Cream the vanilla, cheeses, molasses, and honey (on low speed if you're using an electric mixer). Add 1 cup of yogurt and continue to cream until smooth.

Pour the cooled gelatin mixture over the cheese, stirring constantly. Add the second cup of yogurt. Mix well. Pour into the baked graham-cracker crust and chill until firm.

When you are ready to serve, sprinkle the top with extra graham-cracker crumbs.

GRAHAM-CRACKER-CRUMB SHELL

24 graham crackers, finely rolled (about 2 cups)
¼ cup butter, softened
¼ cup sugar

Preheat oven to 375 degrees.

Blend together the crumbs, butter, and sugar. Set aside ½ cup of the crumbs for garnish. Press the crumb mixture firmly against the bottom and sides of a greased 10-inch pie plate. Bake for 8 to 10 minutes. Cool.

YOGURT CAKE CASSEROLE

What a surprising delight! It's not too bland, not too sweet, but oh, so tart and tempting!

3 cups sifted flour
1 Tbs baking powder
¼ tsp salt
¼ cup butter, softened
2 Tbs grated orange rind
4 cups confectioners' sugar
3 eggs
1 cup plain yogurt, well stirred
2 tsp aromatic bitters
   apricot sauce (recipe opposite)

Sift together the flour, baking powder, and salt; reserve. In a large bowl, cream butter and orange rind until light and fluffy. Mix in sugar. Beat in the eggs, one at a time. Mix in the yogurt and bitters. Stir in the dry ingredients and mix well.

Pour batter into a greased and floured 11-by-17-by-2-inch Pyrex dish. Bake in a 350-degree oven for 40 to 50 minutes. Cool and cut into squares. Spoon the apricot sauce over the squares.

APRICOT SAUCE

2 cups yogurt
12 ounces apricot preserves
½ tsp aromatic bitters

Combine the yogurt, apricot preserves, and bitters.
Beat until smooth.

YOGURTY APPLE SQUARES

A Yogurty Apple Square a day may not keep the doctor away, but you won't care.

½ cup apple juice
2 envelopes gelatin, unflavored
1 cup boiling water
2 cups Dutch-apple yogurt
¼ cup honey
½ cup walnuts, chopped, or raisins

Pour the apple juice into a large bowl and sprinkle in the gelatin. Add the boiling water and stir until the gelatin is completely dissolved.

Whisk into this mixture the yogurt and honey. Pour into an 8- or 9-inch baking pan and sprinkle with the walnuts or raisins. Chill until firm. Cut into squares and serve.

JAMAICAN FROST

Fruit can be used in many delightful ways, but in no more delightful way than in this yogurt-and-gelatin mold.

2 16-ounce cans fruit cocktail
4 cups plain yogurt, well stirred
1 6-ounce package lime gelatin
¼ tsp peppermint extract
    lime slices, for garnish

Drain the fruit cocktail. In a saucepan combine 1 cup yogurt and the gelatin. Cook over low heat, stirring constantly, until gelatin is dissolved. Stir in the remaining yogurt and the peppermint. Chill until almost set. Whip gelatin until smooth and frothy. Place ⅓ cup fruit in an 8-cup mold; fold the remainder into the gelatin. Pour into mold. Chill until it's set. Unmold the gelatin onto a platter. Garnish with lime slices. (Optional flavor: strawberry gelatin may be used instead of lime.)

10 to 12 servings

CHERUB PIE

As lovely as a Valentine and a lot better tasting. Don't wait for February 14 to serve it.

1½ cups chocolate cookie crumbs
3 Tbs melted butter or margarine
1 envelope unflavored gelatin
½ cup cold water
2 cups strawberry yogurt, well stirred
3 egg whites
½ cup sugar

Thoroughly blend together the crumbs and the butter. Firmly press the crumbs into an even layer on the
bottom and sides of a 9-inch pie pan. Chill until firm.
Soften the gelatin in cold water; dissolve over boiling
water in a double boiler. Stir in the yogurt. Chill, stirring occasionally, until the mixture mounds when
dropped from a spoon. Beat the egg whites until soft
peaks form; gradually beat in the sugar until stiff peaks
form. Fold into the yogurt mixture. Pour into the crumb
crust. Refrigerate until set.

6 to 8 servings

STRAWBERRY YOGURT PIE

Perfect for those days when you don't have time to eat, much less cook.

2 cups plain yogurt, well stirred
1 8-ounce or 9-ounce container of Cool Whip
1 10-ounce package frozen strawberries, thawed
1 prepared graham-cracker crust

Fold together the yogurt, Cool Whip, and strawberries. Spoon this mixture into the crust. Freeze 4 hours or overnight. Remove pie and let it stand at room temperature for at least 1 hour before serving.

FRUIT-AND-HONEY
EXTRAVAGANZA

1 11-ounce can mandarin oranges
1½ cups orange juice
2 envelopes unflavored gelatin
2 cups vanilla or lemon yogurt, well stirred
2 Tbs honey
½ cup raisins
½ cup walnuts, chopped
1 cup bananas, sliced

Drain the oranges, reserving the syrup. In a medium saucepan, combine 1 cup of orange juice and the gelatin. Cook over low heat, stirring constantly, until the gelatin dissolves. Stir in the yogurt, the reserved syrup, the remaining orange juice, and the honey. Chill, stirring occasionally, until the mixture is thick but not set. Fold in the mandarin oranges, raisins, walnuts, and bananas. Pour the mixture into a 6-cup mold or into individual dessert dishes. Chill for 3 hours or until firm.

8 servings

FROZEN YOGURT

Lifelong, diehard ice-cream lovers have been known to, overnight and miraculously, become absolute frozen-yogurt freaks. For good reason. Frozen yogurt is almost heavenly in its lightness and pureness of taste.

There are two basic ways to concoct this creamy delight. One is with an ice-cream machine. From the basic recipe all manner of creative variations can be made. The second method uses beater and freezer and nothing else. Both ways result in perfectly scrumptious desserts.

BASIC FROZEN YOGURT WITH ICE-CREAM MACHINE

5 cups yogurt, any flavor (especially good are strawberry, red raspberry, boysenberry, and lemon; vanilla is also quite good)
1 26-ounce box table salt (or as much as your machine instructions call for)
4 trays ice cubes (or as much as your machine instructions call for)
1 cup water, cold (or as much as your machine instructions call for)

Mix the yogurt thoroughly and pour it into the cream can of the ice-cream machine.

Start the ice-cream machine and add up to 26 ounces of salt and the ice cubes in alternative layers. Pour in the water, and in about 30 minutes you will have lightly textured frozen yogurt.

Variations on the Basic Frozen Yogurt Recipe

FROZEN MELBA YOGURT

Follow the Basic Frozen Yogurt with Ice-cream Machine recipe. Use 3 cups peach yogurt and 2 cups red raspberry yogurt.

VERY HEALTHY PARFAIT

Follow the Basic Frozen Yogurt with Ice-cream Machine recipe using strawberry yogurt. When done, alternately layer the frozen strawberry yogurt with a mixture of ¾ cup raisin granola and ¼ cup chopped walnuts.

PEANUT-BUTTER FROZEN YOGURT

4 cups vanilla (or apricot) yogurt
1 cup peanut butter
2 Tbs peanuts (or granola)

Place 1 cup of the vanilla (or apricot) yogurt and the peanut butter in a blender. Blend until smooth. Add the peanut-butter mixture to the cream can of an ice-cream machine and stir in the remaining 3 cups of yogurt. Follow the Basic Frozen Yogurt with Ice-cream Machine recipe.

Serve with the peanuts (or granola) sprinkled on top.

FROZEN YOGURT AMBROSIA

4 cups Dutch apple yogurt
1 papaya, cut in chunks
1 banana, sliced
½ cup shredded coconut, toasted

Place 1 cup of the Dutch apple yogurt in the jar of a blender. Add the papaya and banana. Blend until smooth. Place the remaining yogurt in the cream can of an ice-cream machine and add the pureed fruit. Follow the Basic Frozen Yogurt with Ice-cream Machine recipe. Serve with several spoonfuls of toasted coconut.

LEMON MANDARIN FROZEN YOGURT

4 cups lemon yogurt
2 11-ounce cans mandarin-orange slices

Drain the liquid from the mandarin-orange slices and puree them in a blender. Add the puree to the yogurt and mix thoroughly. Follow the Basic Frozen Yogurt with Ice-cream Machine recipe.

(For a festive dessert, cut a ½-inch slice off the top of a navel orange and scoop out the pulp. Spoon Lemon Mandarin Frozen Yogurt into the orange shells and garnish with fresh mint leaves and fresh orange chunks.)

ORANGE-PINEAPPLE FREEZE

2 cups pineapple-orange yogurt, well stirred
1 6-ounce can frozen orange-juice concentrate,
   thawed
1 tsp grated orange rind
1 Tbs Cointreau (optional)

Combine the yogurt and the frozen concentrate. Add the grated orange rind and (if used) the Cointreau. Pour into an ice-cube tray and freeze. Stir once during freezing.

about 1½ pints

FROZEN BANANA-ALMOND YOGURT

¼ cup cold water
½ cup sugar
¼ tsp salt
1 envelope unflavored gelatin
1 cup ripe bananas, mashed
2 Tbs almond liqueur
1 Tbs lemon juice
1 cup plain or vanilla yogurt, well stirred
2 egg whites
1 banana, sliced

Pour the water, sugar, and salt into a small saucepan and sprinkle the gelatin over it. Set on very low heat and stir constantly until the gelatin is dissolved.

Remove from the heat and add the bananas, almond liqueur, and lemon juice. Stir in the yogurt. Spoon into a loaf pan and freeze for 25 to 30 minutes or until firm.

Transfer the banana-yogurt mixture to a mixing bowl. Rinse out the loaf pan with cool water. Using an electric mixer at high speed, beat in the egg whites. Continue whipping for 8 to 10 minutes until thick and smooth. Return to the loaf pan and freeze until firm.

Shortly before serving, remove from the freezer and allow to thaw slightly. Top with banana slices.

4 to 6 servings

JAMAICAN COFFEE FROZEN YOGURT

Substitute Kahlua for the Tia Maria and it becomes Mexican coffee.

¼ cup water, cold
½ cup sugar
1 envelope gelatin, unflavored
a few grains of salt
1 cup coffee yogurt, well stirred
1½ Tbs Tia Maria coffee liqueur
2 egg whites

Pour the water and sugar into a small saucepan and sprinkle the gelatin over it. Set on a very low flame and stir constantly until the gelatin is dissolved. Add the salt.

Remove from the heat and cool for 5 minutes. Stir in the coffee yogurt and the coffee liqueur. Spoon into a loaf pan and freeze for 25 to 30 minutes.

Transfer the coffee-yogurt mixture to a mixing bowl. Rinse out the loaf pan with cool water. Using an electric mixer at high speed, beat in the egg whites. Continue whipping for 8 to 10 minutes. Return the mixture to the loaf pan and freeze.

DRINKS

BLOODY YOGURT

For all you tipplers, here's a way to have your alcohol without guilt. And if legend is correct, you're drinking your hangover cure with your hangover cause.

1 cup plain yogurt, well stirred
3 cups tomato juice
⅛ to ¼ tsp Tabasco (depending on how much of a kick you need for your spirits to rise)
1 Tbs Worcestershire sauce
¼ tsp pepper
⅛ tsp cayenne pepper
2 jiggers vodka

Combine all the ingredients in a blender and mix for 4 to 5 seconds. Serve with ice.

4 servings

LASSI

This is a variation on a popular Middle Eastern drink. It's sure to conquer the summer heat.

1 cup yogurt
1 cup orange juice
2 bananas, ripe
¼ tsp cinnamon or nutmeg
   honey to taste
4 cubes of ice

Place all the ingredients in a blender and blend until the ice is crushed and the drink is fairly smooth. Pour into glasses.

2 servings

BLUEBERRY SHAKE

It's refreshing, it's yummy, and it's healthy.

2 eggs
2 cups blueberry yogurt, well stirred
1 cup milk
1 tsp aromatic bitters

Place the eggs, yogurt, milk, and bitters into a blender and blend at top speed until smooth. Serve over crushed ice in tall glasses.

4 servings

CREAMY LIMEY LEMONADE

Look! There in the glass! It's lemonade. It's limeade. It's yogurtade! And it's super-refreshing!

1 6-ounce can frozen lemonade concentrate, partially thawed
juice of 1 lime
¼ cup confectioners' sugar
2 cups plain or lemon yogurt, well stirred
2 sprigs fresh mint

In blender container, combine lemonade, lime juice, and sugar. Blend for 3 seconds. Add the yogurt and blend for 10 seconds. Pour into glasses and garnish with mint sprigs.

2 servings

GEORGIA PEACHIE

A drink to make Jimmy Carter feel right at home wherever he is.

½ cup sliced ripe peaches
½ cup cold milk
2 Tbs honey
2 cups peach yogurt, well stirred

Place the peaches, milk, and honey in a blender container. Blend for 10 seconds, add the yogurt, and blend for 10 more seconds.

4 servings

MELON SHAKE

A creamy drink rich enough to be dessert. The next time a craving for a milk shake overwhelms you, forgo the usual mundane concoction in favor of this scrumptious nectar.

1 small ripe cantaloupe, peeled, seeded, and
   coarsely chopped
½ cup cold milk
2 Tbs sugar
2 Tbs lemon juice
2 cups vanilla yogurt, well stirred

Place the cantaloupe, milk, sugar, and lemon juice in a blender container and blend for 10 seconds. Add the yogurt and blend for 10 more seconds.

4 servings

RECIPE INDEX

Index